spring 2015

Mission

We understand "community literacy" as the domain for literacy work that exists outside of mainstream educational and work institutions. It can be found in programs devoted to adult education, early childhood education, reading initiatives, lifelong learning, workplace literacy, or work with marginalized populations, but it can also be found in more informal, ad hoc projects.

For us, literacy is defined as the realm where attention is paid not just to content or to knowledge but to the symbolic means by which it is represented and used. Thus, literacy makes reference not just to letters and to text but to other multimodal and technological representations as well. We publish work that contributes to the field's emerging methodologies and research agendas.

Subscriptions

We are pleased to offer subscriptions to CLJ—two issues per year:

Institutions & libraries	$200.00
Faculty	$30.00
Graduate students & community workers	$20.00

Please send a check or money order made out to the University of Arizona Foundation to:

John Warnock, *Community Literacy Journal*
445 Modern Languages Bldg., University of Arizona, P.O. Box 210067
Tucson, AZ 85721
Info: johnw@u.arizona.edu

Cover Art

Photograph: "Silence/Spaces," by Filippo Minelli. Artist info: www.filippominelli.com

Filippo Minelli started the ongoing series "Silence/Shapes" in 2009 to give a physical shape to silence. As medium to realize his idea he chose chemicals used to create smokebombs and to juxtapose them with the romantic idea of beauty of the natural landscapes.

The use of smoke bomb arose from social and political issues: often used in protests, they generally refer to the imagery of the mass, of bustle, shouting and noise, maybe even violence. But of all this, only one single element remains in the photographs of Minelli, an element that escapes the primary scope of common experience and of its "utilitarian function" to enter the ranks and the modality of what Nathalie Heinich defines in her essay The Sociology of Art as 'objects de regard' or — translated somewhat summary — "objects of the gaze" (a gaze aesthetically addressed, of course). The result is alienating, both at the level of pure visual perception and on the semantic level; Russian formalists would have spoken about disorientation or de-familiarization.

Editorial Advisory Board

Jonathan Alexander	University of California, Irvine
Nancy Guerra Barron	Northern Arizona University
David Barton	Lancaster University, UK
David Blakesley	Clemson University
Melody Bowdon	University of Central Florida
Tara Brabazon	University of Brighton, UK
Danika Brown	University of Texas–Pan American
Ernesto Cardenal	Casa de los Tres Mundos, Managua
Marilyn Cooper	Michigan Technological University
Linda Flower	Carnegie Mellon University
Diana George	Virginia Tech University
Jeff Grabill	Michigan State University
Greg Hart	Tucson Area Literacy Coalition
Shirley Brice Heath	Stanford University
Tobi Jacobi	Colorado State University
Lou Johnson	River Parishes YMCA, New Orleans
Paula Mathieu	Boston College
Regina Mokgokong	Project Literacy, Pretoria, South Africa
Ruth E. Ray	Wayne State University
Georgia Rhoades	Appalachian State University
Mike Rose	University of California, Los Angeles
Tiffany Rousculp	Salt Lake Community College
Cynthia Selfe	The Ohio State University
Tanya Shuy	National Institute for Literacy
Vanderlei de Souza	Faculdade de Tecnologia de Indaiatuba, São Paulo
John Trimbur	Worcester Polytechnic Institute
Christopher Wilkey	Northern Kentucky University

spring 2015

COMMUNITY LITERACY *Journal*

Editors	Michael R. Moore DePaul University
	John Warnock University of Arizona
Senior Assistant Editor	Amanda Gaddam DePaul University
Assistant Editors	Alexandra Nates-Perez DePaul University
Copy Editors	Matthew Fledderjohann DePaul University
	Kevin Kauffman DePaul University
	Kevin Lyon DePaul University
	Margaret Poncin DePaul University
	Bridget Wagner DePaul University
Journal Manager	Daniel James Carroll DePaul University
Design & Production Editor	Aim Larrabee DePaul University
Book & New Media Review Editor	Jessica Shumake Georgia College and State University
Social Media Editor	Melissa Pompos University of Central Florida
Consulting Editors	Eric Plattner DePaul University
	Stephanie Vie Fort Lewis College
	Rachael Wendler Univerity of Arizona

Submissions

The peer-reviewed *Community Literacy Journal* seeks contributions for upcoming issues. We welcome submissions that address social, cultural, rhetorical, or institutional aspects of community literacy; we particularly welcome pieces authored in collaboration with community partners.

Manuscripts should be submitted according to the standards of the *MLA Handbook for Writers of Research Papers*, 7th ed. (New York: MLA).

Shorter and longer pieces are acceptable (8–25 manuscript pages) depending on authors' approaches. Case studies, reflective pieces, scholarly articles, etc., are all welcome.

To submit manuscripts, visit our site—communityliteracy.org—and register as an author. Send queries to Michael Moore: mmoore46@depaul.edu.

Advertising

The Community Literacy Journal welcomes advertising. The journal is published twice annually, in the Fall and Spring (Nov. and Mar.). Deadlines for advertising are two months prior to publication (Sept. and Jan.).

Ad Sizes and Pricing

Half page (trim size 6X4.5)	$200
Full page (trim size 6X9)	$350
Inside back cover (trim size 6X9)	$500
Inside front cover (trim size 6X9)	$600

Format

We accept .PDF, .JPG, .TIF or .EPS. All advertising images should be camera-ready and have a minimum resolution of 300 dpi. For more information, please contact Michael Moore: mmoore46@depaul.edu.

Copyright © 2015 *Community Literacy Journal*
ISSN 1555-9734

Community Literacy Journal is a member of the Council of Editors of Learned Journals

Printing and distribution managed by Parlor Press.

spring 2015

COMMUNITY LITERACY Journal

Spring 2015

Volume 9 Issue 2

Table of Contents

Articles

Collaborative Complexities: Co-Authorship, Voice, and African American Rhetoric in Oral History Community Literacy Projects.................1
Laurie Grobman, Meeghan Orr, Chris Meagher, Cassandra Yatron, and Jonathan Shelton

Digital Literacy in Rural Women's Lives...26
Jennie Vaughn, Allen Harrell, and Amy E. Dayton

Transformative Learning, Affect, and Reciprocal Care in Community Engagement...48
Ashley J. Holmes

Translingual Communities: Teaching and Learning Where You Don't Know the Language... 68
Elizabeth Kimball

Book & New Media Reviews

From the Book & New Media Review Editor's Desk 83
Jessica Shumake
Anthony D. Boynton, II and Saul Hernandez, Interns

Keyword Essay: "Ecology"..85
Janine Morris

After the Public Turn: Composition, Counterpublics, and the Citizen Bricoleur
By Frank Farmer..92
Reviewed by Jason Luther

Phd to Ph.D.: How Education Saved My Life
By Elaine B. Richardson..96
Reviewed by Cynthia Delaney

Del Otro Lado: Literacy and Migration across the U.S.–Mexico Border
By Susan V. Meyers..99
Reviewed by Anne-Marie Hall

New Media Literacies and Participatory Popular Culture Across Borders
By Bronwyn T. Williams and Amy A. Zenger, eds..104
Reviewed by Jessica E. Slentz

Street Sex Workers' Discourse: Realizing Material Change through Agential Choice
By Jill McCracken...108
Reviewed by Angela Clark-Oates

Collaborative Complexities: Co-Authorship, Voice, and African American Rhetoric in Oral History Community Literacy Projects

Laurie Grobman, Meeghan Orr, Chris Meagher, Cassandra Yatron, and Jonathan Shelton

"Between the oral interview and the written manuscript is a long, meandering journey in which a narrative is crafted."

Rebecca Jones

This co-authored article describes a community literacy oral history project involving 14 undergraduate students. It is intellectually situated at the intersection of writing studies, oral history, and African American rhetoric and distinguished by two features: 1) we were a combined team of 20 collaborators, and 2) our narrator, Frank Gilyard, the founder and former director of the Central Pennsylvania African American Museum (CPAAM), was deceased. Because oral history is narrator-driven, Gilyard's death required us to remain especially attentive to the epistemic value of his voice.

Keywords: African American rhetoric; oral history; voice; collaboration; co-authorship; narrative

Introduction (Laurie)

This article is based on the multiple levels of collaboration involved in the written life history narrative of the late Frank L. Gilyard, the founder and former director of the Central Pennsylvania African American Museum (CPAAM) in Reading, Pennsylvania. CPAAM houses art, artifacts, documents, court records, newspapers, and books that focus on local African American history (http://www.cpaam.net/). A collector-based museum, CPAAM opened in October 1998 with approximately 200 pieces from Gilyard's personal collection.

Gilyard passed away on January 24, 2013, prompting me to create this oral history assignment with 14 undergraduates who wrote the narrative as part of a class I taught in spring 2013. The 12 hours of recordings from 2010 were in my possession and in the CPAAM collections. Gilyard and I had been involved in six community-based research and service learning partnerships since 2005. Before his passing, we had planned on two projects for the spring 2013 semester, including this cross-listed upper division English and American Studies special topics course designed around a thorough local African American historical research and writing project centered on videotapes of Gilyard reciting local African American history. His knowledge was encyclopedic, but he always said most of it was in his head, not written down. Gilyard, his wife, CPAAM colleagues, and many African American community leaders had been talking for years about the need to videotape and preserve the undocumented information in Gilyard's memory. These video recording sessions were scheduled for February 6 and 7, 2013, less than two weeks after Gilyard's passing. Students were to use Gilyard's oral historical stories as a foundation for in-depth research; at the same time, the course was focused on rhetorical history, and students would study and produce historical discourse through the lens of rhetoric.

After Gilyard's sudden death, I decided after a great deal of contemplation that the students would write a collaborative oral history narrative based on the existing first person recordings of Gilyard's life (not of local African American history). I had done several previous class projects with local oral histories and was familiar with scholarship and pedagogical practices in the disciplines of both oral history and community literacy projects. Most of the oral histories were conducted by a former student of mine, Jessica Didow, for a graduate school capstone project at a local university in 2010.

Although I knew these were preliminary, not final, recordings, I was certain Gilyard wanted these recordings of his lived experiences publicly shared. That we were 12 days away from videotaping six hours of local African American history was tragic; Gilyard had also spoken many times about having an autobiography written about his life to share with the Berks County community. I felt that creating this assignment for the students would be both a tribute to Gilyard and a gift to his family and the community, and most important given my obligation to my students, an excellent learning experience for them. Further, as Linda Shopes argues, the oral histories of "nonelites" is recognized for their

> potential for restoring to the record the voices of the historiographically— if not the historically—silent ... few people leave self-conscious records of their lives for the benefit of future historians. Some are illiterate; others, too busy. Yet others don't think of it, and some simply don't know how. And many think—erroneously, to be sure—that they have little to say that would be of historical value. By recording the firsthand accounts of an enormous variety of narrators, oral history has, over the past half-century, helped democratize the historical record.

Gilyard knew he had a great deal to say, and he said some of it during the interviews in 2010. In my view, it was important to his legacy and the work to which he committed the final two decades of his life—recovering and preserving local African American history—to share these recordings with a wider public. In this sense, Gilyard was like

Goldie Baker and Shirley Wise, African American activists whose oral histories were documented by Rhonda Williams; Wise and Baker seemed keenly aware of their role and responsibility as speakers of their life histories, family details, and community histories—and the interconnectedness between them all (59). I did not consult with Gilyard's widow, Mildred Gilyard, at the time because she was grieving. However, I knew the written narrative would not be put into the CPAAM collection without her review and consent.

This community-engaged oral history project involving 14 undergraduate students is intellectually situated at the intersection of writing studies, oral history, and African American studies. In this article, I, three students from the class (Meeghan, Chris, and Jonathan), and a staff assistant (and former student of mine), Cassandra, who served as an editor, write about the many complexities of this multilayered oral history.[1] Two features of this oral history project make it distinct and, therefore, offer important insights about collaboration, voice, and African American vernacular in oral history and community literacy projects: 1) that we were a combined team (including the late Gilyard) of 20 collaborators, and 2) that our narrator, Gilyard, was deceased. Because oral history is narrator-driven, Gilyard's death required us to remain especially attentive to the epistemic value of his voice. This article begins with my discussion of context and pedagogy. Next, Meeghan, Chris, and Jonathan focus on the issue of voice in two ways: through the collaboration of the 14 students and in trying to capture and preserve Gilyard's voice. Cassandra, who had known Gilyard and spoken with him one-on-one several times, analyzes her role as an insider and outsider editor. Ultimately, we argue that this collaborative oral history project informs theory and practice of collaboration in oral histories, in community literacy projects, and in undergraduate writing instruction.

Pedagogical Approach (Laurie)

Teaching this course in the immediate aftermath of Gilyard's death inevitably brought many pedagogical challenges. I was relatively experienced with teaching oral histories in both first year composition and introductory literature classes, although in these courses, students conducted the interviews themselves. I was also experienced with community-based undergraduate research projects. Since 2005, students and I have worked closely with the African American community, through and with the local NAACP branch and the Central Pennsylvania African American Museum (CPAAM) in Reading; the Hispanic/Latino community(ies), through and with Centro Hispano Daniel Torres, Inc.; and the Jewish community, through and with Jewish Federation of Reading and Jewish Cultural Center of Reading. Furthermore, my scholarly work had by then been informed by rhetorical performance and blackness. As students were conducting their work, I was simultaneously writing a now-published article about Gilyard's rhetorical performances of blackness in the founding of CPAAM (Grobman).

First, I had to help students transition from a "doing history with a foundation of oral history" to a "doing oral history" mindset. By the time of Gilyard's passing, students had read Leon F. Litwack's *How Free is Free?: The Long Death of Jim Crow* (2009) for its revisionist history through deeply felt oral performance and storytelling. Litwack argues that economic inequalities are less visible but "far more intractable" (120) than legalized segregation had been, but whites' resistance to economic equality has perpetuated and reinforced racial injustice. I assigned *How Free is Free?* as a way to provide students with a foundation for the local African American historical work they would be doing, beginning with videotaped recordings of Gilyard that were to take place. Litwack employs a collage of many black voices—including excerpts from journalism, novels, poems, songs—and many oral histories of everyday, "ordinary" people, such as porters, maids, and military personnel. He pieced together many excerpts from oral histories and interviews (most that had been published elsewhere) as well as used other secondary and primary sources to create a larger historical narrative covering more than a century. For many students, Litwack's book was their first exposure to oral history and to African Americans' fundamental contributions to a revised, expanded version of the American history master narrative.

Students in my class would now be using existing audio recordings to write a narrative of one man's life. Oral history interviewing is "first and foremost a historical endeavor" (Noriega and Bennett 2), a "genre specifically designed to discover what individual experience means in historical terms" (2). We were seeking to understand, and to convey, how Gilyard's lived experiences fit within the larger historical context, both contextualized and localized. By then, I was familiar with much of the scholarly work on African American oral histories in the disciplines of both oral history (Rose; Williams)[2] and composition and rhetoric (Carter and Conrad; Carter and Dent; Coogan). But I wanted to find something closer to the complicated work we were to embark on regarding collaboration, co-authorship, and voice. As Gregory Zieren asserts, oral history pedagogy typically involves a "triangular relationship between instructor and student, between student and interview subject, and even between instructor and subject" (158). But these students did not conduct the interview they would collectively transcribe and use as the basis for a narrative. Furthermore, students would work in several reconfigured pairs and small groups from transcription through revision.

Rebecca Jones's article in *Oral History Review* was an excellent departure point for these students. Jones claims that "The oral history interview is the starting point in the process of creating the narrative, but the journey continues through transcribing and editing to publication" (23-24). Jones discusses her work as writer/editor of *Blended Voices: Kingston Residents Tell Their Stories of Migration* (City of Melbourne), a book based on oral history interviews with migrants living in the Kingston area of Melbourne, Australia. The book is largely a group of first person narratives, mainly in English, except for ten of the stories, which are reproduced both in English and in the narrator's native language. Jones, who was historian, interviewer, editor, and writer, turned the transcripts into a written narrative, what she calls the "edited story" (27). Changes were made after narrators reviewed the stories, and a professional copy editor "corrected punctuation and typing mistakes, and made minor changes in phraseology" (27).

Jones's analysis focuses on transforming a verbatim transcript into a narrative, arguing that "editing, extracting, refining, and rearranging the transcript" is "part of the joint construction of a narrative by both the narrator and the writer/oral historian in which a public text is created from a private one-to-one conversation" (24). "Joint construction," Jones asserts, is "influenced by the power relationships inherent in oral history and governed by ethical responsibilities" to the narrator, audience, content and context of the stories, and the project's purpose (24). "Editing *Blended Voices*," according to Jones, "involved extensive condensing and manipulation of the text" (27); among the more substantive changes she made include removing passages that did not relate directly to the issue of migration and settlement, reordering phrases so that the same themes appeared together and cut repetitions, and creating paragraphs. Most importantly regarding the issue of voice, or "blended voice," the term Jones uses in the titles of both the book and the scholarly article about the book, was that Jones "rendered the resulting stories in something close to Standard English" (27) by altering grammar, syntax, and punctuation. Jones states that she attempted to "retain idiosyncrasies of speech" and "reproduce[e] the lilt and cadence of the participants' speech" (27). Jones provides the following example of Ahmed, who migrated to Australia in 1992 from spending his youth in Harar, Ethiopia. His first language is Amharic. Jones first reprints this passage verbatim from the transcript and then the edited version:

Unedited

I'm going to drop out and work in a factory because I have no choice, no I didn't. I know I'm going to go through with it, and if I don't go through with it I keep questioning myself, how did he make it? I'm not stupid. I can think. I can communicate. There's nothing wrong with me, I could do it, I could just keep pushing myself. I never gave up in anything because life is experience, it is a test whether you pass or fail. (33)

Edited

Sometimes I found things so difficult that I thought I would just drop out of school. But I didn't. I kept questioning myself and pushing myself. I knew I wasn't stupid and so I never gave up. Life is an experience and a test. (33)

Jones acknowledges that "Ahmed's phrasing has been considerably altered" but also claims that "we have remained true to the meaning of his story and communicated it in a way that is accessible to the intended audience" (33). She asserts that it "illustrates the barriers to understanding created by faithful reproduction of the spoken word" (33). My reaction was that Jones had gone too far in the direction of erasing her narrators' voices (the vast majority of the students agreed with my reaction). That was my starting point for the oral history narrative project. How would 20 collaborators, including 14 students who had never met Gilyard and did not conduct the interviews with him, create and maintain his voice while writing a third person narrative from more than 12 hours of recordings?

I assigned readings that would inform students' work with principles of collaboration, co-authorship, and voice in the disciplines of writing and rhetoric, oral history, and African American studies. In addition to Jones's notions of "joint construction" and "blended voice," students read about collaboration and narrator-centric oral histories through "Principles for Oral History and Best Practices for Oral History" (Oral History Association) and "Transcribing Oral History" (De Blasio). "What They Do: How the Co-Authors View their Collaborative Writing Process," a chapter from *(First Person)2: A Study of Co-authoring in the Academy* (Day and Eodice), offered perspectives on students working in teams as well as on collaborative concepts such as negotiation, compromise, shared voice, and shared vision. I selected "African American Orality: Expanding Rhetoric" (Garner and Calloway-Thomas) because it is an accessible and good overview of some of the most salient features of African American rhetoric. Students were journaling throughout the process, connecting the readings and their work collaborating with one another and with Gilyard and Didow through the interviews. Alessandro Portelli asserts, "Oral history … refers [to] what the source [i.e., the narrator] and the historian [i.e. the interviewer] do together at the moment of their encounter in the interview" (qtd. in Shopes). In the Frank Gilyard oral history narrative, there were many moments of encounter. The process and timeline of the project with its many layers of collaborators were as follows:

Stage 1: Recordings: Frank L. Gilyard, Narrator, and Jessica Didow, (Interviewer Summer 2010). Didow visited and spoke to the class on February 7, 2013.

Stage 2: Transcription of recordings, students (February 7-20, 2013)

Stage 3: Deciding how to craft and organize the narrative, students and Laurie (February 21, 2013)

Stage 4: Drafting the narrative, students (February 22-March 16, 2013)

Stage 5: Revising the narrative, including initial review and question and answer session with Van and Mildred Gilyard, students (March 17-March 26, 2013)

Stage 6: Editing the narrative: Cassandra and Laurie (March 27-April 27, 2013)

Stage 7: Second review by Van and Mildred Gilyard (April 27-May

Stage 8: Final editing (Laurie) and transfer of narrative, transcripts, and recordings to Mildred Gilyard, CPAAM.

The interviews were the foundation of the collaboration that was to come. I was a co-interviewer for one of these sessions for the project I was doing. When Didow and I conducted the interviews, we were committed to the Oral History Association's "Principles and Best Practices for Oral History" that "include commitments to the narrators, to standards of scholarship for history and related disciplines, and to the preservation of the interviews and related materials for current and future users" (1).

Didow visited my class in early February 2013 to discuss some of the more relevant issues that students needed to know to transcribe and write the narrative oral history.

Two primary issues stuck out as challenges for the students' work. First, Didow stressed to students that the interviewing "felt unfinished." She explained, "I was going to send [Gilyard] the transcriptions, and he was going to look over them, and then we were going to continue interviewing." In my interview with Didow, she developed this point:

> There never was an end. Like each time that I interviewed him, the end was decided by the clock, so we talked for the duration of time that we had set aside ... we never really had an ending where he got to say, 'I said everything that I wanted to say,' or, 'I wish I hadn't said that. Please don't include that.' Or anything like that because I was going to go back to him.

Chon Noriega and Teresa Barnett suggest that oral historians usually seek "a narrative, not just discrete answers to a set of questions" (3); Didow explained to the students that she gave Gilyard free reign to tell her what he wanted, and then she was going to go back to him for further questioning: "He mostly talked and I listened. If there was something that I felt that I knew at the time that I would need clarification on I asked, but mostly he was talking and I was listening." They ended each interview "knowing that they weren't really over."

I was aware that the interviews were not completed, and the decision to use the existing recordings was not made lightly. Being unable to follow through with Gilyard to fill in the gaps and clarify what we may have misinterpreted presented an ethical as well as practical dilemma. Was it fair to Gilyard that he would not be able to review the narrative? Review by the narrator is "standard practice" for oral history (Jones 34); through review and revision, the narrator "continue[s] to construct the narrative" (36). Furthermore, even though I knew Gilyard had wanted his story shared, "it is only at the time of the review, when the narrator sees a manuscript that might be published, that he or she considers the story as a public text" and seriously considers revision (Jones 35). In her discussion of the editor's responsibility, Jones cites Alistair Thomson's comment that "oral histories 'from below' which have been written by researchers 'from above' can be disempowering for the objects of research" (qtd. in Jones 37); the unequal power dynamic was made extraordinarily sensitive due to Gilyard's passing. His voice was limited to the transcript and our interpretation of the transcript. In Jones's book, six out of 39 participants amended their stories because they realized the repercussions of public voicing (36).

Ultimately, because I was confident Gilyard wanted his life history shared, I was comfortable with the decision to go forward. As Shannon Carter and James Conrad assert, "People exist amid a constant flow of competing narratives, places, time constraints, and obligations. We capture what we can, always aware that we can never capture everything; thus, our records are always partial, inadequate interpretations rather than reliable, complete, unbiased and unfiltered historical records" (98). Carter and Conrad's oral history project involved interviews with dozens of local African American citizens across three generations in the Norris community, a rural town in northeastern Texas, to have archives available for future research. They are aware that in so doing, the narrators may be deceased, but their recordings will live on, despite being partial. And these recordings are critical to a comprehensive and inclusive historical record.

The second primary concern for students raised during Didow's visit to the class was that she conveyed to them that even hearing Gilyard's voice did not fully capture the conversations or the person behind the voice. Rhonda Williams's article in *Oral History Review* focuses on the performative aspects of oral histories, emphasizing interviews she conducted with Shirley Wise and Goldie Baker, two black female public housing residents who have been tenant activists in Baltimore since the 1960s. Interestingly, Williams never explicitly discusses the use of African American Vernacular English (AAVE) in the interviews, but Meeghan, Chris, and Jonathan will raise this issue as it pertains to the Gilyard oral history in their analysis. Rather, Williams cites Elizabeth Tonkin's concept of "Voice," emphasizing the significance of performance in oral history: "Gesture, intonation, bodily stance and facial expression are all cues, in the oral ambience, to topic orientation as well as to the speakers' claim to authority" (qtd. in Williams 44). Williams further develops this notion: "Voice, then, not only represents the spoken words in narrative, but also how those words are performed" (44), and Voice "can unveil layers of knowing" (45). I quote Didow at length on this point:

> I'm not sure if his humility comes across in the transcripts ... When he talked about other people in the museum and other people in the community he was very proud of them and really animated and excited to know this information and found this information and share it with someone else. And when he spoke about himself, he never seemed to put himself in the same category of a community leader or community hero or someone that was making a contribution or going above and beyond that he thought that these other people were. He just spoke about himself very matter-of-factly...You're missing like the essence of his being, kind of, like in the physical way. Like his calm presence and his mannerisms and the amount of respect that he had for humanity in general and people ... I think that not getting to see his face when he talks about the things that he's talking about, while I said that he was less animated, you could definitely read on his face there were times that brought him a lot of joy or other times that were harder for him that I'm not sure if that would come across in his tone of voice as much as it did in his body language and facial expressions.

Like Williams, Susan D. Rose omits all discussion of AAVE in her chapter describing an undergraduate project at Dickinson University to conduct and preserve oral histories of the local African American community. The first stage of interviewing took place in 1989-1990; the second phase in 2001 was a broader historical study on the African American community in Carlisle, PA and included a diverse group of students from Dickinson, Dillard, and Xavier universities. Students used the 1989-1990 oral histories and conducted new interviews as part of this project. Rose's article emphasizes the interaction between students and narrator. She argues that the project fostered in students more complex understandings of race and other categories of difference. However, there is no discussion of AAVE or voice.

However, I was also committed to acknowledging and honoring AAVE as an explicit feature of Gilyard's voice. As a writing scholar-teacher, I have long been concerned with teaching students about the complexities involved with language, race, and power.[3] I have written elsewhere about the African American oral tradition's influence on Gilyard's speech (Grobman). Like E. Patrick Johnson's grandmother, whom he describes in *Appropriating Blackness: Performance and the Politics of Authenticity*, Gilyard "draws on [his] cultural and experiential knowledge" of black vernacular traditions and "internally dialogizes them" (Johnson 153). Gilyard, a deeply religious man who was integrally involved in his church on local, state, and national levels, was influenced, like Johnson's grandmother, by the "repetition and rhythm [that] are integral to the preacher's performance style" (153). These upper-division students in the American Studies major and Professional Writing major were already familiar with the consensus among linguists that AAVE involves a set of rules that are distinct from, but not inferior to, those of Standard Written English. A "subsystem of English" (Bailey 287), AAVE developed concurrently with the early 20th century "great migration" of African Americans from the rural South to the urban North (Wolfram 111). As Meeghan, Chris, and Jonathan write about in the next section, Gilyard's African American voice was one of many challenges they and their classmates confronted while writing the narrative.

Collaboration, African American Rhetoric, and Voice (Meeghan, Chris, and Jonathan)

We—Meeghan, Chris, and Jonathan—are three students from the course in which 14 students co-wrote the written narrative history of Gilyard. None of us had ever been involved in oral history until this experience, but when Gilyard died, we felt that doing this project would be an important contribution to this man's life history and work. We never met him, but by that time in the semester, we knew enough about him and felt Laurie's sense of loss to know writing this oral history would be a tribute to his memory.

As three of the 14 undergraduate collaborators, we faced several challenges. Our focus in this article is on the concept of voice from two perspectives: 1) how 14 student collaborators achieved what rhetoricians Kami Day and Michele Eodice call "joint voices" (129); and 2) how 14 student collaborators worked to preserve Gilyard's voice, according to what oral historian Jones refers to as "blended voice."

In rhetoric and composition, the issue of voice in writing has been studied by many scholars. Tom Romano states that "voice is the writer's presence on the page… Voice is the human quality of written language that is directly related to its sibling, the spoken word" (50). This human quality was to be found in the merged voices of

Gilyard, the interviewer, 14 students, and two editors. According to Peter Elbow, "the voice lens highlights how language issues from individual persons and physical bodies and how the same words differ, depending on who says them and how" (175). Students had to convey Gilyard's voice lens—Gilyard's "language as sounded, heard, and exiting in time" (175)—through our individual and collective voice lenses without having ever seen his physical body. Thus we had to find a way to convey the sound of Gilyard's voice through writing.

Joint Voices: Collaboration with 14 Students

Kami Day and Michele Eodice's book, *(First Person)2: A Study of Co-authoring in the Academy*, discusses several concepts related to the collaborative work in Gilyard's written oral history narrative. They define co-authoring as "working together—topic and idea generation, research, talk, possible co-writing, decisions about how the final product will look, etc. on a writing project" (121-22). Chris and Jonathan had co-authored before, but Meeghan had not. When we read Day and Eodice, Chris and Jonathan agreed that their past experiences in co-authoring were developed well through practice in previous writing classes. Meeghan had concerns about her lack of experience co-authoring and her writing ability in a group of students majoring in writing. She was uncomfortable with the process, but working with her peers who had more experience was essential to the success of her writing. We knew from Day and Eodice that "more planning goes into a co-authored piece" than when writing alone (127) and that "a great deal of talk, which involves negotiation and invention that leads to decision-making" would be required of all of us (127). After each stage of transcription, writing and editing, the class had come together to decide as a group how the narrative should be structured, framed, revised, and edited. We had several decisions to make: which elements of Gilyard's life were important enough to keep, how to structure the narrative, and finally, who was going to write the sections before we could then take on the challenge of Gilyard's voice. From transcribing and deciphering Gilyard's words to the final edit of the narrative, every step of the process was carefully chosen and directed by the students.

The class split into groups for our first drafts. By working with others on this narrative, multiple interpretations, ideas, and opinions were necessary to consider before moving forward with any writing. After transcription, our job was to decide how to craft and organize the narrative (referred to earlier as Stage 3). Laurie's instructions for us were to collaborate, negotiate, and make decisions about the following:

1. "In ranked order, at least three proposed ways of structuring and organizing the narrative.

2. The rationale for each structure/organization.

3. The assigned sections for each pair or small group (no more than 3) writers.

4. Any large chunks of material you think should be omitted from the narrative."

Day and Eodice interviewed co-authors who described their talk and realized it had brought them rewards. For them, "their talk was epistemic in that they learned more about each other and about what they do, and what's more, they had fun" (130). While our groups may have had fun, it certainly wasn't without its conflicts. In this stage of our narrative, some of the decisions Laurie required us to make were very difficult. For instance, we argued over the sections of the narrative and whether chronological order was important. We also struggled with assigning groups as there were some students who did not articulate what sections they wanted to work with. Chris and Meeghan finally spoke up, however, and told our classmates that the decisions needed to be made; we presented our vision of the structure, and the groups finally agreed. In the end, it was an "epistemic," or knowledge-making, experience as the group negotiated through several iterations and agreed on a plan that made the most sense at the time: four sections including Race, Racism, and Race Relations; Military; Early Childhood; and Work Life. Kara was the designated spokesperson for the class. She told Laurie our chosen topics along with our chosen groups. In a response later that day, Laurie wrote the following email to students.

> Great job! I agree with your "theme" structure but am adding both "Religion" and "Race, Racism, and Race Relations." Religion is so important to the Gilyards that I think it must be included as a separate theme. Race, Racism, and Race Relations are so important to Frank's life that I want to begin by separating this out as a separate theme. As the narrative takes shape, we will decide whether to leave it as interwoven into other ideas or to separate it out as its own chapter/theme.

As we recall it, none of the students, ourselves included, were upset by this decision since Laurie knew far more about Gilyard and his life than we did.

It was time to begin Stage 4, which was Drafting the Narrative. During class on February 26 we divided the first draft of the narrative into these groups and topics:

- Childhood: Kara and Erin

- Military Life: Chris and Jeff

- Museum: Bianca and Seth

- Race: Meeghan, Liz and John

- Religion: Ed and Nate

- Work Life: Lauren and Brittany

These groups made their own decisions about what should or should not be included in the section. Each group interpreted the transcriptions and chose the ways in which they wanted to write a section of the narrative and what parts of the interview to include and exclude.

Collaborating on a narrative by writing independently and in small and changing groups may seem disjointed, as students Ed and Nate point out in their co-authored essay: "Of course there was no blueprint to follow, no guidelines to structure our process, the nebulous quality of this process is described by Jones when she wrote that, 'There is no definitive formula for creating a written manuscript from oral interviews; a different project may require different decisions to be made'" (25). Ed and Nate also summarize some of the most challenging issues for us as we worked together to write the narrative: "Indeed, each [narrative] is its own. In fact, ours was more greatly complicated by the following factors: first, that Gilyard was not with us to help us; second, that Jessie's interviews, though good, had a different goal than we did; and third, that there were so many student writers with different ideas and backgrounds and opinions." In our view, Didow's interviews, while conducted for a different purpose, provided enough material to gather a good, although incomplete, narrative of this man's life. Also, while there were obvious difficulties in dealing with the opinions of 14 students, it was to be expected and all decisions were handled in a professional manner with all parties being satisfied. Gilyard's death, however, left many unanswered questions and gaping holes in the narratives that were inevitably filled with the authors' interpretation of his reality.

Meeghan, Jonathan, and another student, Elizabeth, worked together on the section about race and race relations. We worked, as Day and Eodice claim, using the "partial collaboration" method (131). We never sat down and wrote face-to-face, but instead each took a small section and wrote individually. We then tried to blend our sections together. While this seemed like a good idea at the time, due to the timing of each of our writings, we were left scrambling to blend our sections together. This part of the process did not lead to our best writing. Chris and Jeff, however, worked face-to-face, what Day and Eodice call "full collaboration" (131). Chris and Jeff's process was closer to that described by co-authors Emily Hui and Roja Grant in Day and Eodice's study: one writes a draft (for us, a section of a draft), then the other works on it, and so forth, and we also sit and work together (131). For example, Jeff would write a section, and Chris would reword, or even rewrite, that same section.

After about two weeks, we merged all subgroup sections into a full narrative and began Stage 5, Revising the Narrative. Laurie posed the following questions for us to think about as we approached this phase of revision:

- Are there overarching themes, issues, motifs?

- How should we shape and structure?

- Where are there overlaps and repetitions?

- Should race, race relations, and racism be interwoven in pertinent sections or its own section (or both)?

- Are there inconsistencies to address, and if so, how?

- What specific tasks do you see yourself doing at this step?

These posed questions were intended for us to decide what the narrative needed and how to make it more concise and direct. For example, our primary decision was to integrate religion and race/racism into the four other sections. At this point, everyone, including Laurie, agreed that the structure would change from six to four topics, leaving only Childhood, Military Life, Work Life, and the Museum, which would each be written chronologically. Because race/racism and religion were so integral in everything Gilyard did and said, to make these into separate categories would be to separate the very core of Gilyard himself. We also determined that Gilyard's voice needed to be more prominent in the narrative. Each group of writers then had to incorporate more quotes from Gilyard. We needed some clarification and additional information, so two students, Lauren and Nate, went to CPAAM to meet with Mildred and Van Gilyard

As we began this stage of revision, Meeghan, Chris, and Jonathan felt a sense of disconnection. By that point, each group had become "author-ities" of its section, but Laurie reconfigured our groups to try to give us a different perspective on how the narrative was being written. We felt that the narrative read like a mish mash of fourteen students' writing rather than a cohesive piece. As Romano explains:

> There are many kinds of written voices. I've read those that were raucous and spirited, like a roaring fire. I've read voices subdued and sincere, like a coffee shop after morning rush. I've read voices so aloof and distant, so abstractly intellectual and fraught with jargon that the writing was impenetrable, like an unyielding, brick wall. I've read voices that are windy and cluttered with wordiness and qualifications. And I've read student voices riddled with spelling aberrations, nonstandard usage, and incorrect punctuation, yet the meaning of the words was unmistakable, the presence of the writer undeniable. (51)

The written voices in our narrative at this point were as diverse as Romano describes. In particular, some writers in the class struggled at this point in the narrative to establish their own presence among the stronger writers. Often, the stronger writers would rewrite sections written by classmates.

But soon we began to collectively work on the narrative to establish the "joint voices" we were so desperately after. In order to ensure that every author understood the direction of the narrative at all times, in depth discussions were necessary during class time. It was at these moments when the students came together to blend their voices that the narrative was formed. Kara felt that the narrative was co-authored in its entirety. She states in her essay, "Many of our class periods were devoted to in-depth discussions of how different elements would be combined to create the final narrative. While every member of the class wrote a different part of the narrative… we constantly had to come back together as a class to make sure all elements of the document worked in tandem with each other." While we worked in small groups much of the time, collaborative group work as a whole was essential to the blending of the narrative. These larger group conversations were epistemic in that each idea elicited further and different ideas. By the time we handed over the narrative to Laurie and

Cassandra, some of the students, including Meeghan and Chris, were not fully satisfied that we had achieved the joint voice we were seeking. However, Laurie felt that it was time for an editor, Cassandra, to bring the voices further together, and that the students had to move on to reflective and analytical work on the narrative project.

Blended Voices: Gilyard's Voice

Simultaneously with joining the voices of 14 students, we were mindful at all times of blending this joint voice with Gilyard's voice. Jones uses the term "blended voices" in both the title of her book and her article analyzing her book. Although she never explicitly defines the term, she implies how as a writer and editor, she must blend her voice with that of her narrators.

> The principle that motivated these choices is an understanding of editing as part of the joint construction of a narrative by both the narrator and the writer/oral historian in which a public text is created from a private one-to-one conversation. The joint construction is, in effect, a relationship between narrator and writer influenced by the power relationships inherent in oral history and governed by ethical responsibilities. In editing oral history, we, as authors, have to balance responsibilities to the narrator, to the audience, and to the content of the stories. The decisions we make in balancing these responsibilities are dependent on the purpose of the project. (24)

Our goal, indeed our obligation, was to share Gilyard's story rather than our interpretation of his life. But the issue of Gilyard's voice was a constant tension. We and our classmates were attentive to the issue of erasing the oral history narrator's voice after reading Jones's article. As Laurie wrote earlier in this article, almost every student in the class felt that Jones erased too much of the narrator's voice in her article. Rather than blending voices, we felt she had erased voices.

Shopes asserts that during the interview, "the voice of the narrator literally contends with that of the historian for control of the story." At this point in the collaboration, we viewed our work to retain Gilyard's voice as cooperation, not control. We struggled to keep the group's voice cohesive and readable while attempting to blend it with Gilyard's to ensure that his voice was the dominant presence.

Among the most significant issues was that Gilyard's African American Vernacular English was at times challenging for us to follow. 13 students were white, and one was mixed race Hispanic and black; more importantly, we were college-level juniors and seniors and well versed in standard written English. We agreed with Jones's point that "when publishing for a general audience, extensive editing is necessary to create a document that is not only readable and accessible, but also conveys the flavor of the experiences" (26). But what did "extensive editing" mean? How much was too much? Donna DeBlasio states that a narrative should "reflect the speaker's character and preserve as much of the quality of interview as possible yet still be readable" (108).

Several students expressed our common concern. Lauren states, "as Jones says, I don't want to "increase the distance between the reader and narrator by removing too much." Scott struggled with keeping Gilyard's voice as unfiltered as possible. He explains, "a lot of phrases and concepts have been awkwardly translated, including my own. I feel that a lot of the narrative's integrity has been lost simply due to Gilyard's unique way of speaking, a way that can't be replicated well in written form." What transpired was a melding between Gilyard's spoken African American Vernacular English with the students' carefully crafted, written academic vernacular, leaving not much of either. So we continued to seek a better balance.

Very little research exists explicitly discussing AAVE in oral histories. David Coogan's article describing a service learning project during which students conducted oral histories of residents in Bronzeville, an African American neighborhood in Chicago, is primarily focused on the notion of civic dialogue. The article references AAVE only once, when an African American student in the class, Danielle, was criticized by one of the narrators, Deborah, for what Deborah believed was a misrepresentation of the Bronzeville residents that would perpetuate negative stereotypes. Danielle had transcribed the interview literally, and many of the stories in the publication were uncensored; she had also "'intended on speaking with her'" before the journal went to publication (105). Deborah told Danielle that although she and her husband are educated, the printed oral history makes them "look ignorant" (105). Danielle reflects on the experience, realizing that she and her classmates unwittingly conveyed the impression "'that all blacks speak a certain way'" (105). Coogan asserts that what bothered Danielle the most was that she "failed to deliberate meaningfully with Deborah about representing her side" (105). Quite obviously, we would never have that opportunity with Gilyard, although the final reviews and decisions were made by his widow and son. But Gilyard signed consent forms in the many projects Laurie did with him giving his permission to quote him directly. Yet how would we remain faithful to his voice?

Williams, an oral historian, never explicitly discusses the use of AAVE (African American vernacular English) in the interviews she conducted with African American women, even though AAVE is apparent in their transcripts. For example, in the following excerpt from Goldie Baker's interview, Williams discusses Baker's laughter as a way to convey irony:

> Honey, that's when I went to see the commissioner. And I told him, I don't know who he [Newton] think he's talking to. I am not nobody's slave. I AM NOT no-BODY's SLAVE, and he AIN'T talking to no slave, slavery's over … I said he don't have no respect for me, he don't need to be over there. He don't need to be no manager.
>
> And then the rest of the residents start telling me about (voice lowers), "Oooh, girl, how you talked to him like that?! Don't you know you'll get put out!"… And that's what got me concerned. 'Cause I said, oh, no, unh-unh, nobody is supposed to talk to you, talk down to you like, who they think they are? They

work for you! [...] You pay his salary. Girl, people thought I was...I thought like they was going to hog tie me out of there ... I did not know that our people were so afraid to talk to white people [referencing the commissioner] until I really got involved. But now, then, I understood why my mother and them was fighting for rights, for so-called human rights for poor people. (55-56)

Williams indicates that in the excerpt, bold represents louder; she does not mention capital letters (53); furthermore, the insertions about lowering of voice and laughter are hers. In our view, some of the power in Baker's story comes through her very powerful voice as Williams transcribes it verbatim and with clues to intonation and syntax. We could picture this woman speaking, her body movements and facial expressions, and we are confident that some features of AAVE are part of the power of Baker's voice.

Two readings in our course assisted our efforts to retain Gilyard's voice. Litwack's *How Free is Free?: The Long Death of Jim Crow* is African American history from an African American perspective using African American voices. Litwack's academic voice controls the narrative to an extent, but the book is filled with examples of famous and ordinary African Americans telling their stories. Litwack made certain that their voices were seen, heard, and understood, providing for readers interpretations of those who experienced firsthand the events. For hundreds of years, whites have been providing their interpretation of historical events. We learned from Litwack that African Americans have used oral history throughout the centuries to intervene in discourses that have marginalized and erased them; therefore, oral history is of critical value to documenting and preserving African American history. From Garner and Calloway-Thomas's "African American Orality: Expanding Rhetoric" we learned "the space between the rhetorical practices of African Americans and the landscape of African American orality" (44) is critical to understanding Gilyard's narratives. We were able to link many of the features and characteristics of an African American oral tradition to Gilyard's voice, in particular, the "unrehearsed" quality of Gilyard's storytelling (50), such as when Gilyard abruptly changed the topic from boot camp, to a dispute he'd had with a fellow soldier, to a discussion of running in the heat. Sometimes we lost track of where he was going with his stories, but we came to realize why this "improvisation" (50) was such a profound feature of the recordings. In the end, we are confident that we honored Gilyard's voice to the extent possible under the circumstances.

Insider/Outsider: My Role as the Editor (Cassandra)

My role, like the others in this project, does not fit neatly into the categories of oral histories. As an editor, my job was to edit the narrative for an unfamiliar reader while also unifying the voice of the narrative. In addition to issues raised by Jones, I turn to Deborah A. Gershenowitz's "Negotiating Voices: Biography and the Curious Triangle Between Subject, Author, and Editor" and her role as editor of two oral history-based biographies, Catherine Fosl's *Subversive Southerner: Anne Braden and the Struggle for Racial Justice in the Cold War South* (2002), and Sandy Polishuk's *Sticking to the Union: An Oral History of the Life and Times of Julia Ruuttila* (2003). Gershenowitz's situation and role were quite different from mine in many ways. She is a professional editor for Palgrave Macmillan, and she is writing about the "curious triangle" (71)—subject, author, editor—of published oral history-based biographies. Gershenowitz's focus is on her role as a "detached outsider that intrudes on a very intimate relationship" that has been established between writer and subject (72), and her main argument is that the editor's outsider role is what enables her to effectively fulfill her role as editor, negotiating that "rocky terrain that oral history-based biographers navigate with their editors, subjects, and perhaps most importantly, their own voices and agendas" (72).

My role as editor was somewhere between outsider and insider. That is, I had not interviewed Gilyard for this project and therefore, like other editors, did not have what Gershenowitz refers to as "an intimate relationship" between author and subject (72). Yet, I was not an outsider, nor did I feel like an "intruder" (72). I knew Gilyard; I had spoken to him and worked with him one-on-one several times in the few months before his death, as recently as mid-December, a month before he passed away. Thus, it was both my insider and outsider status that guided my editorial decisions to unify the voice of the writers, maintain both Gilyard's voice and readability for a general public, and make Gilyard's life meaningful in a local historical context.

At the time of this oral history narrative project, I was the program assistant for the Center for Service Learning and Community-Based Research at Penn State Berks; Laurie is coordinator of the Center. Among my primary duties was to assist faculty and students conducting service learning and community-based research. But Laurie also wanted me on this project because I had known Gilyard and had spoken with him and listened to him tell personal and historical stories. I had first met Gilyard in spring of 2009, when he spoke to my general education Alternative Voices in American Literature course, taught by Laurie. Recently, as the program assistant for the Center, I had the opportunity to work with him closely and speak to him directly. For a Fall 2012 Honors first year writing class, the students conducted research on local history subjects suggested by Gilyard. He provided a folder literally bursting with newspaper articles and photographs that he had found in the local libraries' archives and at the Bethel AME Church and that people had given to him over the years. For a few hours, Gilyard and I discussed which people or events he thought the students should research, such as people who had interesting stories or significant events in local and national history that he believed should be remembered. We also went through photographs from the church where he identified every person he could remember, which was a surprising number of people. I had visited the museum three or four times, sometimes with Laurie and sometimes alone. But I had known him a much shorter time than Laurie, and while I developed a relationship with him within those four months, it was not the kind of emotional bond Laurie had with him. Therefore, I had a level of distance she did not have; I also had a level of familiarity the writers did not have.

Laurie sent me the narrative with the students' separate sections combined into one piece. By then, I had listened carefully to the recordings and read through the full transcript several times. The students who wrote the narrative could hear Gilyard's voice in the recordings but not see the gestures or facial expressions he used when telling stories. Every time Gilyard and I had met, he had a new story or fact to share with us about local history. Because I had seen him tell stories quite a few times, I could visualize his hand gestures and facial expressions in the recordings, which became more animated when he told a story. Gilyard would hunch his back and lean forward when telling a story, and I would find myself leaning in to listen and hear every word.

My simultaneous tasks were to unify the third person voice, maintain or make Gilyard's voice prominent, and establish Gilyard's life as significant both personally and historically. As Gershenowitz writes, editors and writers work together to "convince readers—many of whom have never heard of the subject—that the life ... *is* history" (73, emphasis in original). I consulted the writers for information and clarification, but I was given the authority from Laurie to make the changes I thought should be made and to track all changes for her review and consideration. I also made comments for writers and Laurie throughout the narrative.

The students transcribed the recordings verbatim, but for the narrative, we would not use first person (as Jones did), and therefore the third person narration would need to be balanced with direct quotations from Gilyard. Our goal was to stress "the orality of the source" (Jones 32). I had briefly studied AAVE and the oral tradition in an American literature class in college. Presently, I found Jacqueline Jones Royster's article, "When the First Voice You Hear Is Not Your Own," helpful in understanding why it was so important that we retain Gilyard's storytelling voice in the narrative, given the historical reality of slavery, Jim Crow, and racial discrimination. Oral history and storytelling are vitally important to African-based cultures, which we wanted to honor in our narrative. For far too long, Royster argues, African American voices have been "muted" (36). About her own role as a negotiator across cultures, Royster writes that at times,

> I speak, but I can not be heard. Worse, I am heard but I am not believed. Worse yet, I speak but I am not deemed believable. These moments of deep disbelief have helped me to understand much more clearly the wisdom of Audre Lorde when she said: "I have come to believe over and over again that what is most important to me must be spoken, made verbal and shared, even at the risk of having it bruised or misunderstood" ... Lorde teaches me that, despite whatever frustration and vulnerability I might feel, despite my fear that no one is listening to me or is curious enough to try to understand my voice, it is still better to speak. (36)

Royster argues that the "challenge is to teach, to engage in research, to write, and to speak with Others with the determination to operate not only with professional and personal integrity, but also with the specific knowledge that communities and their ancestors are watching" (33). It was incumbent on us to speak *with* Gilyard, not for or about him. Within academia and society, we need to "articulate codes of behavior that can sustain more concretely notions of honor, respect, and good manners across boundaries, with cultural boundaries embodying the need most vividly" (33). Stories are vehicles for theory and lessons, and through the manipulation of storytelling, one becomes "a performer" (35). As storytellers, we needed to enact Gilyard's performance, to evoke emotion and memories and tell his stories his way. Royster makes it very clear that neither she nor other African Americans speak in only one "authentic" voice (37). We were striving for the voice he uses in the interviews, without denying Gilyard's multiple voices. Laurie had made it very clear that in the time she had known him, Gilyard took control of his voice and performance depending on circumstance and situation. As an African American man living through Jim Crow, segregation, and subtle and overt racism, Gilyard had to use false voices that were not his own. Yet, as Royster says about herself, "when the subject matter is me and the voice is not mine, my sense of order and rightness is disrupted" (31). Our job was to adhere to Gilyard's storytelling voice in the interviews to honor him and to affirm his lived experience both personally and historically.

Most of the third person voice in the narrative was consistent; however, in the section titled "Childhood," the style was distinctly different from the other chapters. Although in third person, the narrative read like this:

> When his brother got out of the Second World War, he put a light up there in the stairwell above the door. Up the stairwell was one room in the back filled with big trunks and a closet. This was the first room. The front room was the bedroom. It had and old bed with springs and under each mattress and springs was an old Sunday school quarter. It was a bible and it was turned open under the bed, face down. This was because it would keep the witched and haunts away. They would go away because they didn't like scriptures. This was an old custom of the South.

I think the students were attempting to recreate Gilyard's voice in third person, but that did not work as far as readability, clarity, or authenticity. I re-read the transcript, and revised the passage to read this way:

> When Frank's brother came home from fighting in World War II, he put a light in the stairwell above the door. Up the stairwell, there was one room in the back filled with big trunks and a closet. The front room was the bedroom fitted with an old bed with springs. Under the mattress, they placed an open Bible face down, which is a Southern superstition that was supposed to keep witches and ghosts away.

I removed the words that Gilyard used in speech or words one would use if speaking in person, such as "there." I could imagine Gilyard using his hands to demonstrate where the light used to hang, but that does not have the same impact when reading the narrative or if a reader never met Gilyard. When explaining a fact of a story or setting the scene, Gilyard would use short sentences because he would ask the person if they understood what he was saying. It reads, "Up the stairwell was one room in the back filled with big trunks and a closet. This was the first room. The front room was the bedroom." Gilyard spoke like this, but for a reader, it is a bit jarring and confusing, so I changed it to read, "When Frank's brother came home from fighting in World War II, he put a light in the stairwell above the door. Up the stairwell, there was one room in the back filled with big trunks and a closet." It lacks the flavor of Frank, but it is more concise and clear. This was more the student speaking like Gilyard, than an actual quote, so it did not feel as if I were removing Gilyard.

Throughout the editing process, I attempted to keep the meaning of Gilyard's stories. When editing certain sections, I tried to read it to myself with Gilyard's enthusiasm and expressions in mind, and then to sound like him without taking on a false AAVE. For example, I wrote, "Although Frank's family was not wealthy, he said they "'weren't *poor* poor,'" and he was able to save money from his shoe shining job to travel with Mr. Farmer and his boys' club." In the transcript, he said these exact words "'we weren't poor poor'" with an emphasis on the first "poor." The tone on the first "poor" implies a meaning that his family did not have money to waste but they weren't destitute. Their basic needs were met. I inserted quotations when I wanted to reference his tone of speech within the narrative or if he stated an opinion or personal judgment. I never intentionally changed the meaning of his words and stories, and if I had a question, I asked the students or Laurie if they knew what he was trying to say.

I also reorganized some paragraphs and stories to improve the flow of the narrative. Gilyard was a gifted storyteller, and I tried to show that in the structure of the narrative. Gilyard's interviews were like the one-on-one conversations we'd had; he starts off and goes off in tangents of other stories or ideas. As a class, we discussed arranging the narrative like one of Gilyard's stories, but the students decided that ordering each section chronologically would be the clearest way of telling his story. The content within the chapters starts out being chronological in most of them, but sometimes branches off to tell small stories and then comes back to the main subject. One change I made in several places was to move pieces to other paragraphs because they complete a story or explain what Gilyard may have been referencing in another.

During the final edit, Laurie asked me to carefully consider whether the narrative was missing any stories I thought should be included, and I suggested the story about his father's ghost because it adds "the flavor of [his] experiences" to the overall narrative (Jones 26). I had known Gilyard briefly and heard him tell stories; now I appreciated the opportunity to listen to his interviews and to learn about his personal life and a deeper glimpse into his past. It was also important to me to share Gilyard's stories with the public.

Conclusion: "our own very personal marks"

Meeghan and Chris: Through several revisions and a lot of group work and consultation, we are confident that the final version of the written narrative captures Gilyard's voice. Of course, we missed out on knowing Gilyard personally and on being able to talk with him about the written narrative. We didn't have the luxury of knowing what Gilyard would prioritize; we had to decide for ourselves. In doing so we formed a man's history for him and without him, leaving our own very personal marks in the writing. We did this, of course as Anna Hirsch and Claire Dixon assert, because we were writing creatively and out of necessity, and we were seeking to "represent truth" (189). This is not necessarily a bad thing. As writers of this narrative we had to work "creatively and systematically to construct or invent an imprint of life that is as lifelike as possible" (189). Our goal was to depict Gilyard's life, his struggles, as accurately, authentically, and vividly as possible; we had to invent a way to retell his story as best we could.

Laurie: Meeghan and Chris's paragraph above speaks to me on several levels. It reminds me that they and their classmates never had the privilege of meeting Frank Gilyard, yet he was able to accomplish what he had done so many times before: provide students with a substantial learning experience while simultaneously recovering, preserving, and disseminating local African American history. It reminds me of the creativity, intelligence, courage, and integrity of Meeghan, Chris, their classmates, and the many students who embark with their faculty and their communities on community literacy projects. And it reminds me of why we must continue to reach across boundaries to implement community literacy projects, despite all of their challenges, leaving all of "our very own personal marks" in our communities. In "Life Changing Assignment," a poem she wrote for her final writing project in the class, Elizabeth Boulanger captures the power of Frank Gilyard's life and students' collaboration with him:

> Walking into a new class,
>
> Not knowing what to expect,
>
> Seeing old and new faces.
>
> We hear of a man,
>
> A man of inspiration,
>
> Who impacted our city greatly,
>
> And changed lives.
>
> Setting up interviews with him,
>
> The worst news fell upon us.
>
> We hear of his departure,
>
> And of his family's despair.
>
> Unable to fully understand,
>
> We became intrigued by his life,

Discovering his voice from the past,
We were able to hear his tale.
For the first time he came to life.
We were able to understand,
And see our town from a new point of view.
He spoke of two wars,
A war of the nations,
And a war back home.
He made the pain feel real,
And the struggle came off the pages,
As we jotted down every spoken word.
In class we spoke of what we heard,
And put the puzzle together,
Creating a memorial for him.
After knowing his story,
His wish became our desire.
We wanted the community to remember,
Remember what he did for them,
And made a change in the city.
Writing his story was an experience,
We grew as a class,
As writers, and as friends,
But not just academically.
We got to know Frank,
His story, his family, and his town,
Having a story come to life,
About the struggles
Faced by the Afro-Americans,[4]
And altered our world for the better.

Endnotes

1. We received Institutional Review Board approval to conduct this study. All students who remained in the class gave permission to use their real names and to quote from their written materials. I have used pseudonyms for the two students who participated in transcription but then dropped the course. Jessica Didow gave permission to quote from her interview.

2. Susan D. Rose describes an undergraduate project at Dickinson University to conduct and preserve oral histories of the local African American community. The first stage of interviewing took place in 1989-1990; the second phase in 2001 was a broader historical study on the African American community in Carlisle, PA and included a diverse group of students from Dickinson, Dillard, and Xavier universities. Students used the 1989-1990 oral histories and conducted new interviews as part of this project. Rose's article emphasizes the *interaction* between students and narrator. She argues that the project fostered in students more complex understandings of race and other categories of difference. However, there is no discussion of AAVE or voices.

3. I am always cognizant—and open with students and the Gilyards—about the implications of white academics writing about black individuals. In the many partnerships between the Gilyards, me, and my students, the Gilyards have authorized us to speak.

4. Gilyard regularly and intentionally used the term "Afro-Americans."

Works Cited

Bailey, Guy. "A Perspective on African-American English." *American Dialect Research.* Ed. Dennis Preston. Philadelphia: John Benjamins, 1993. 287-318. Print.

Barnett, Teresa, and Chon A. Noriega, eds. *Oral History and Communities of Color.* Los Angeles: UCLA Chicano Studies Research Center Press, 2013. Print.

Carter, Shannon, and James H. Conrad. "In Possession of Community: Toward a More Sustainable Local." *CCC* 64.1 (2012): 82-106. Print.

Carter, Shannon C., and Kelly L. Dent. "East Texas Activism (1966–68): Locating the Literacy Scene through the Digital Humanities." *College English* 76.2 (2013): 152-70. Print.

City of Kingston. *Blended Voices: Kingston Residents Tell Their Stories of Migration.* Melbourne: City of Kingston, 2001. Print.

Coogan, David. "Community Literacy as Civic Dialogue." *Community Literacy Journal* 1.1 (2006): 95-108. Print.

Day, Kami, and Michele Eodice. *(First Person)2: A Study of Co-authoring in the Academy.* Logan: Utah State UP, 2001. Print.

DeBlasio, Donna M. "Transcribing Oral History." *Catching Stories: A Practical Guide to Oral History.* Donna M. DeBlasio, Charles F. Ganzert, David H. Mould, Stephen H. Paschen, and Howard L. Sacks. Athens, OH: Swallow, 2009. 105-13. Print.

Didow, Jessica. Personal Interview. 31 May 2013.

Elbow, Peter. "Voice in Writing Again: Embracing Contraries." *College English* 70.2 (2007): 168-88. Print.

Garner, Thurmon, and Carolyn Calloway-Thomas. "African American Orality: Expanding Rhetoric." *Understanding African American Rhetoric*. Ed. Ronald L. Jackson II and Elaine B. Richardson. New York: Routledge, 2003. 43-55. Print.

Gershenowitz, Deborah A. "Negotiating Voices: Biography and the Curious Triangle between Subject, Author, and Editor." *Oral History Review* 32.2 (2005): 71-76. Print.

Grobman, Laurie. "'I'm on a Stage': Rhetorical History, Performance, and the Development of Central Pennsylvania African American Museum." *College Composition and Communication* 65.2 (2013): 299-323. Print.

Hirsch, Anna, and Claire Dixon. "Katrina Narratives: What Creative Writers Can Teach Us about Oral History." *Oral History Review* 35.2 (2008): 187-95. Print.

Johnson, E. Patrick. *Appropriating Blackness: Performance and the Politics of Authenticity*. Durham: Duke UP, 2003. Print.

Jones, Rebecca. "Blended Voices: Crafting a Narrative from Oral History Interviews." *Oral History Review* 31.1 (2004): 23-42. Print.

Litwack, Leon F. *How Free is Free?: The Long Death of Jim Crow*. Cambridge: Harvard UP, 2009. Print.

Noriega, Chon A., and Teresa Barnett. Introduction. Barnett and Noriega 1-18.

Ritchie, Donald A. *Doing Oral History: A Practical Guide*. Oxford: Oxford UP, 2003. Print.

Romano, Tom. "Writing with Voice." *Voices From the Middle* 11.2 (2003): 50-55. Print.

Rose, Susan D. "'It Wasn't a Sweet Life': Engaging Students in Oral History Interviewing across Race, Class, and Generations." Barnett and Noriega 76-97.

Royster, Jacqueline Jones. "When the First Voice You Hear Is Not Your Own." *College Composition and Communication* 47.1 (1996): 29-40. Print.

Shopes, Linda. "Making Sense of Oral History." *History Matters: The U.S. Survey Course on the Web*. Web. 2002. 15 Dec. 2013.

Williams, Rhonda Y. "'I'm a Keeper of Information': History-Telling and Voice." *Oral History Review* 28.1 (2001): 41–63. Print.

Wolfram, Walt. "The Grammar of Urban African American Vernacular English." *Handbook of Varieties of English*. Ed. Bernd Kortmann and Edgar Schneider. Berlin: Mouton de Gruyter. 111-32. Print.

Zieren, Gregory R. "Negotiating Between Generations: A Decade of Teaching Oral History." *Oral History Review* 38.1 (2011): 158-74. Print.

Author Bios

Laurie Grobman is a Professor of English and Women's Studies at Penn State Berks. She is the 2014 Carnegie Foundation for the Advancement of Teaching Outstanding Baccalaureate Colleges Professor of the Year. Grobman's teaching, research, and service interests center on community-based research and multicultural education in writing and literary studies. Grobman has published two single-authored books, three co-edited collections, including the recent *Service Learning and Literary Studies in English* (MLA 2015) and several articles in journals such as *College English, College Composition and Communication*, and *Reflections*. She also has one forthcoming co-edited collection: *Pedagogies of Public Memory: Teaching Writing and Rhetoric at Museums, Archives, and Memorials* (Routledge 2015). Grobman is a co-founder of *Young Scholars in Writing: Undergraduate Research in Writing and Rhetoric* and the founder of Undergraduate Journal of Service Learning and Community-Based Research.

Meeghan Orr graduated from Penn State University, Berks in December 2013 with a BA in American Studies. Meeghan and her co-authors presented this research to the Penn State University, Berks Advisory Board on March 20, 2014 and at Northeastern Modern Language Association's annual conference in Harrisburg on April 3, 2014. Meeghan has followed her passion for herbalism and started her own business, Wise Oak Herbs, where she crafts herbal medicines for her local community.

Chris Meagher is currently a student in the professional writing major at Penn State Berks.

Cassandra Yatron graduated from Penn State University in 2012; she is scheduled to teach English in Korea beginning in August 2015.

Jonathan Shelton graduated from Penn State Berks in 2013 with a B.A. in professional writing. He is currently attending law school.

Digital Literacy in Rural Women's Lives

Jennie Vaughn, Allen Harrell, and Amy E. Dayton

This qualitative study looks at how rural women in the American South have obtained access to digital technologies for reading and writing. Using the "life history" approach (Brandt; Hawisher and Selfe), we interviewed five women. We look at the challenges caused by the Digital Divide, at economies of access, including the financial factors that shape individuals' uses of digital technologies for reading and writing, at the strategies that the women used for gaining access to needed technologies, and at the nature of sponsorship in digital, rural contexts.

Keywords: literacy; rural; women; digital divide; technology; access; sponsorship; qualitative

Introduction

In 2014, the World Wide Web marked its 25th birthday.[1] The Pew Research Center observed the occasion with a report showing how drastically the Web has changed the lives of individual Americans. In 1983, several years before the World Wide Web was born, only 10% of adults had a home computer. Today, 81% of adult Americans regularly use computers, 87% use the web, and 68% use "smart" mobile devices (e.g., phones or tablets with Internet access) (Fox and Rainie). Although access to the Internet has increased for many Americans, rural households are less likely to have access than their urban counterparts. This gap in Internet access has increasingly become a focus of the federal government. The Clinton administration coined the term "digital divide" to describe the gap between those who have access to emerging technologies and those who do not, and initiated the "Falling Through the Net" project (1995-2002) to track computer ownership and network access across broad demographic categories. By contrast, the Bush administration suggested that the digital divide was no longer a significant problem (Grabill; Ruecker). The Obama administration, however, believes that the problem persists, and therefore has focused on connectivity in schools. The ConnectEd initiative seeks to provide access to 99% of America's students by upgrading Internet connections, training teachers, and encouraging private sector innovation ("ConnectEd"). Due in part to these federal initiatives, as well as to changes in consumer habits, more Americans use digital technologies for literacy today than ever before.

While rates for computer and Internet usage are climbing, reliable access to the Internet continues to be problematic, in part because the gap is narrowing in unequal ways (Besser; Grabill). For this reason, scholars such as Todd Ruecker suggest that the "digital divide" must be understood not as a simple binary (whether individuals have access to digital technology) but rather as a multifaceted concept that includes consideration of "not only type of access but the way individuals have developed technological literacy through self-sponsorship or sponsorship by another figure, such as a teacher, in a way that enables them to more effectively contribute to societal discourses" (Ruecker 241). As Jeffrey Grabill puts it, "what we miss when we focus [solely] on the statistics is that access is deeper than simple infrastructure … access is a moving target" (462). Moreover, as Howard Besser argues:

> though the gap in technological access has narrowed, other critical gaps still remain … between those who have the skills and competencies to effectively evaluate the appropriateness of a given piece of information, and those who do not. A major divide still remains between those able to apply critical thinking and evaluation to an information source and those who cannot.

At the national level, then, scholars and policy makers increasingly recognize that digital literacy is important to the lives of American people, and that access to digital technologies is an especially important issue for Americans in isolated communities.

These broad changes in technology, access, and federal policy create the backdrop for this study, which looks at how women in the American South have obtained access to digital technologies for reading and writing. Using the "life history" or "literacy narrative" approach (Brandt; Hawisher and Selfe; Ruecker), we interviewed five rural women, asking, in part, how has technology shaped your reading and writing practices? How have you gained access to technologies for literacy, and how have you learned to use them? We were interested in how issues of access affect rural people—though we tried, in approaching our topic, not to presume that participants and their communities would be deficient in their access to or use of technologies. The lives of the women we interviewed, whose ages range from their early 30s to mid-40s, have been shaped by the technological revolution of the 1980s, 1990s, and the new millennium. They have seen the emergence of new technologies that include the home computer, the Internet, Web 2.0, and, more currently, smartphones and wireless devices, which are changing the ways people access and produce texts. Though we would not attempt to draw general conclusions based on our small sample, we do offer a look at the particular, local dynamics of these five cases, whose experiences are unique to them, yet part of broad social and technological trends that are still unfolding as we write this.

Background and Methodology

The question, "What is rural?" confounds nearly everyone who works with rural populations of the United States. According to the US Housing Assistance Council, rural areas share the characteristics of having comparatively few people living in an area, but they differ in their proximity to urban areas, community size, total population, population density, and other social and economic factors (Housing 8). Policy makers often view the concept of rural through an "urban-centric perspective; thus, many definitions focus on urban and metropolitan areas, and other territory is classified as rural by default" (Bucholtz 30).

In fact, determinations about what counts as "rural" are often rhetorical, made for particular purposes and contexts. Federal agencies—such as The United States Office of Management and Budget (OMB), the United States Census Bureau, and the United States Department of Agriculture—classify areas as rural (or not) in order to make determinations about funding and about the regulation of industry and land management. Official determinations vary by agency and by purpose for classification. Due to the variable nature of official classifications, the rural population of the US can be considered as low as 17% or as high as 49%. This variation "reflects the reality that rural and urban are multi-dimensional concepts, making clear-cut distinctions between the two difficult" (Bucholtz 29). In other words, although rural areas have a rich culture and history in the United States, the concept of *rural* is shifting and unstable.

In their book, *Rural Literacies*, Kim Donehower, Charlotte Hogg, and Eileen E. Schell point out that much of the previous research in community literacy has been "skewed toward urban sites and subjects. Many of our theories and research paradigms presume an urban or semi-urban setting and do not account for the experiences and realities of rural places and peoples" (12). The authors call for scholarship that addresses this gap and counterbalances the "deficit model of rural life that is commonly perpetuated in academic scholarship and popular press and media representations. All too often, life in rural America is seen as 'lacking:' lacking education, lacking economic opportunities, lacking cultural opportunities." At the same time that the authors caution us to avoid stigmatizing rural communities and individuals, they also seek to avoid painting romantic, sentimental views of rural communities (14). In thinking about how we have framed our study of rural women, we might add that rurality, while of course a central aspect of this project, is nonetheless only one aspect of our participants' lives, and a complex one at that; moreover, the distinctions of "rural" versus "urban" are not always clear cut. For instance, two of our participants, while strongly identifying themselves as rural people, have spent significant portions of their lives in urban areas, for their jobs and for their education.

We chose to focus on rural *women* for several reasons; first, due to a desire to uncover the voices of those who are mostly likely to be silenced or left out of official accounts of literacy practices. Beyond this impulse, however, we note that women most often perform the role of initial literacy sponsor (for their children, for instance) and make many decisions regarding the purchase and use of technology within the home. The women we interviewed were instrumental in selecting and purchasing the computers and other devices that their families use for reading and writing. Their influence spread as they and their family members ventured into the community.

Moreover, by virtue of their role as librarians and teachers, several of the women play a special role in sponsoring the literacy of other members of their communities. By talking to them about the many contexts in which they read and write, we attempt to show the multifaceted nature of women's writing rather than limiting the focus to the domestic or the family sphere.

We were interested not only in our participants' contexts for digital literacy, but in the *kinds* of literacy they exhibit. In his book, *Multiliteracies for a Digital Age*, Stuart Selber outlines three categories of computer literacy that are essential for adequate participation in the digital age: *functional, critical,* and *rhetorical. Functional computer literacy* positions the computer as a tool and the student as a user whose objective is effective employment of the tool (25). *Critical computer literacy*, in Selber's framework, places the student as questioner of technology with the objective of performing an informed critique of the computer as a cultural artifact (25). In this category the user is critically engaged in recognizing and questioning "the politics of computers" (75). Selber argues that critical literacy allows technology users to "work against the grain of conventional preoccupations and narratives, implicating design cultures, use contexts, institutional forces, and popular representations within the shape and direction of computer-based artifacts and activities" (95). In other words, with critical computer literacy, users are engaged critics, not passive consumers. Finally, *rhetorical computer literacy* is a category that involves the creation of twenty-first century digital texts. Being rhetorically literate in the digital age involves more than just creating content, but involves consideration of interface, web design, the connectivity and usability of hypertexts, and so on.

Our study uses the "life history" interview approach, which we have adapted from Deborah Brandt, as well as from Cynthia Selfe and Gail Hawisher. Our purpose was to learn more about the "cultural ecology" of literacy—the range of social, cultural, economic, and personal factors that shape individual reading and writing practices. In her groundbreaking book, Literacy in American Lives, Deborah Brandt notes that this research method, in the tradition of oral history, emerges out of an interdisciplinary framework that includes "historical, sociological, psychological, and phenomenological inquiry...What these diverse traditions have in common is an interest in people's descriptions of their own life experience" (10). Inspired by Brandt's project, Cynthia Selfe and Gail Hawisher embarked on a study using the life history approach to explore Americans' life histories as they related to literacy and technology. Emerging in the early 2000s, their work captured the experiences of the first generation of Americans who experienced technological revolution of the 1980s and 90s. In their article in *College Composition and Communication*, the authors summarize the key findings of that study (also detailed in their book, *Literate Lives in the Information Age*). We quote them at length here, as they provide key insights into the nature of digital literacy: 1) "Literacies have life spans." 2) "People can exert their own powerful agency in, around, and through digital literacies." 3) "Schools are not the sole—and often, not even the primary—gateways through which people gain access to and practice digital literacies." 4) "The specific conditions of access have a substantial effect on people's acquisition and development of digital literacy." 5) "Families transmit literacy families and practices in multiple directions" (644). As we reflect on our interviews, we consider how our interviewees exert agency through digital literacy, how they acquired literacy inside and outside of school, how access affected their literacy development, and how their family literacy practices worked in multi-directional ways.

After obtaining permission for the project from our institutional research board, we located our participants, with Amy reaching out to her former writing students, and Allen and Jennie contacting members of their communities. The study included two initial steps—a background questionnaire that asked for demographic information and general information about the participants' reading, writing, and technological habits, and a structured interview in which we asked participants how they learned to read and write, how they learned to use computers, how they get access to the technology they need in their daily lives, and how they use digital literacy for specific contexts—academic, professional, public (as in, for church or community groups), and personal.[2]

After we gathered and transcribed the interviews, we developed a set of analytical categories to analyze the transcripts. Some of the categories—such as "rurality," or "sponsorship," were part of the study from the outset, but others, such as "anxiety about technology" or "resourcefulness," emerged as we coded the interviews. We used a two-step process in which each interview was read and coded twice. In keeping with the life history approach that Brandt, Selfe and Hawisher pioneered; we sought to create research partnerships with our interviewees, who are participants, rather than "subjects," in this project. All of our participants have chosen to use their real names and have had the opportunity to read, respond, and reflect on our draft. In this way, they can be part of the process of analyzing and making sense of the data we gathered. As we explain in the next section, this project comes out of our commitment to rural people and places and to democratic, participatory research methods.

The Researchers' Stance

Jennie: My interest in this project stems from the intersection of my personal and professional lives. As a feminist scholar of writing, rhetoric, and literacy, I focus on work done by ordinary women in their everyday lives. I hope to broaden the scope of the field by (re)valuing the work and influence of women, often overlooked by the academy and the historical record. Acknowledging the value of women's literate practices in the home and community can help to reframe the ways we think about and teach literacy, writing, and rhetoric.

Personally, I identify as a woman from a rural community. I currently live in the same small town as my two interview participants. They are women I know and admire. We have worked together over the years as community and school volunteers. I have been connected to or living in this community for over 25 years. I can relate to our participants' struggles to gain, maintain, and afford reliable Internet access. I am, in many ways, the population this study seeks to examine.

Allen: In my graduate-school coursework, I focused on issues affecting rural populations, as I had recently moved back to my childhood home after living 16 years in Birmingham, Alabama, my state's largest city. I immediately understood that the access I had taken for granted while living in "the city" was the stuff of dreams in "the country." I became interested in issues of access as a larger problem in all rural areas after reading a *New York Times* article that focused on the town and the public school at which my grandmother taught for 39 years and from which most members of my family graduated (Severson). The article focuses on the struggles rural students and community members face without fast and reliable Internet access. Since the article's publication, the county board of education closed the school, and the town is dying. I believe that Internet connectivity and access to the information, goods, and services found online are important not only to a community's longevity but also to the fate of all rural people. And as an instructor at my local community college, I witness the challenges that a lack of access to technology creates for my students. Therefore, I believe that in order for future generations of rural Americans to remain in these areas or to survive in the world outside of them, rural people must have reliable broadband Internet access or they will be left behind.

Amy: Since coming to work at a large public university in the Deep South, much of my teaching has made use of oral history as a primary research method. In spring 2012, I taught a graduate-level course on research methodology, in which Jennie and Allen were enrolled. This project emerged out of our conversations and interests in rurality and digital literacy, women's literacy practices, and the potential for the life history approach to help us gain insights into these issues. As a faculty member at a large institution that has increasingly moved to attract out-of-state students, I feel a personal commitment to better understand a group of students who are less visible on our campus—nontraditional, local, and especially, rural students.

Participants

We chose to focus on adult women, and on literacy success stories rather than on focusing on the deficiencies of rural people or rural communities. Indeed, all of the women we interviewed are highly literate: skilled at reading and writing in a variety of contexts. Patricia and Rhonda are librarians at small public libraries. Connie co-owns a home-photography business, volunteers in the community, and recently began homeschooling her son. Kody and Kristy are returning college students who have recently finished their degrees, and Kody is a homeschooling mom. As librarians, Rhonda and Patricia are community literacy sponsors in their libraries—a technological gateway. As president of the local library board, Connie is connected to community literacy, too. As mothers, all five women serve as literacy sponsors (digital and otherwise) within their families as well. Aside from being digitally literate, these women lead lives rich with reading and writing experiences.

Case Studies

Connie Ford is a white, married mother of two. At age 43, she lives with her family in Ragland, AL, a small town of about 2,000 residents. This is also Connie's husband's hometown, and her in-laws and large extended family live here, too. She is active in the local community, serving as president of the board of the local public library and as an officer of the local school's parent-teacher organization. While Connie has worked out of the home over the years, she currently runs a photography business from home with a partner as she homeschools her thirteen year-old son. Her sixteen year-old daughter attends the state school of math and science and now lives at the school (four hours from the family's home). The family uses technology extensively for school, work, communicating, and entertainment. Each family member has an Apple iPhone, which serves as the primary device for much of their digital literacy practices including: texting, Internet surfing, gaming, posting on social media, and reading. Also, the family owns two desktop computers used primarily for school.

Connie describes herself as "a pretty voracious reader" and says she has been since she was young. In fact, she remembers surprising her grandparents by reading to them at age four: "They thought that I had just memorized the book, but I was actually reading." As a young reader, Connie found her family to be a supportive and attentive audience. She notes, "Reading as a whole was just a really profound thing for me as a kid. My parents were divorced when I was a year old … My mom worked, she was a single mom for a long time, and I think reading was just an escape for me." Connie also connects her early experiences with reading to her love of libraries saying, "The library was such a cool thing for me as a child. I loved to go there, and books were just special. I just always had a sense [that] books were something to be revered." At the same time, Connie associates books with adventure and taboo, saying, "Because I was a curious and interested and bright child, I really just read everything I could get my hands on. I probably read things I shouldn't have at that age." Today, both paper and digital texts play an important role in her life. She spends about twenty-one hours a week engaged in some sort of reading activity including reading novels, magazines, newspapers, emails and texts, social networking messages, the Bible, and her son's homeschool assignments. Admittedly, Connie spends less of her time engaged in writing activities, but she spends anywhere from four to seven hours a week writing emails, texts, notes for her son's homeschool lessons, to-do lists, and social networking messages.

Like most of our participants, Connie has lived both with and without digital technology. She did not use computers in high school or college and laughs about her college paper-writing experiences, "I guess I just handwrote [papers]. What an archaic thing to do!" Her first experience with a computer was at her first job as a teenager in the late-1980s, "I remember inputting data. And I can remember it was so slow that I kept a book with me and I would just read until it processed … it was ridiculous!" After that, more than a decade passed before she purchased a home computer. By then she was married with a young daughter. Connie laughingly remembers her initial skepticism about digital technology, "I can remember, you know, people talking about the Internet, and being like, 'What is that? That just sounds too much to bother with.'"

Today, digital technology is an integral part of Connie's life. She spends at least forty-eight hours a week using some sort of digital device like her desktop, smartphone, or smart television. Functionally speaking, she conducts much of the work for her photography business on the computer, both online and offline. She edits photos, orders prints, communicates with clients, and advertises her services digitally. Her son's homeschooling curriculum is computer-based, and she uses Internet sources to supplement his learning. Connie engages with these sources critically, noting, "You do want to verify and make sure that what you just read is accurate. If you can get three places that say the same thing then you're fairly certain." She continues, "Well, I think you definitely err on the side of caution … just because you found it on the Internet absolutely doesn't mean that it's true." As for her rhetorical digital literacy practices, Connie has used a DIY hosting service to create a website for her company, and she frequently posts both personal and professional content on Facebook. Though she uses her desktop computer for paying bills, editing photos, homeschooling, and sending emails, Connie relies most heavily on her smartphone because "It's just so much easier." With her daughter living hours away at school, Connie feels that mobile devices keep her family connected.

Looking back, Connie admits that her family's first technology purchases were based more on advertising, noting that they bought a Gateway desktop because "Gateway was just a highly advertised brand … a little bit more well-known to us." However, over the years she and her husband have become more savvy and resourceful technology consumers learning to shop for specifications and capabilities over name brands. She says, "I think that as you use [computers] more and you get more comfortable with the technology … enough to know that it's all the same components … You can find out exactly what it is that you're getting, it doesn't matter what brand it is."

This same resourcefulness is again evident when Connie explains her family's experiences in gaining, maintaining, and financing Internet access. She describes her options for Internet access as "very limited" and often expensive. Currently, the family has DSL service through the local, privately-owned telephone company. Connie notes that she has tried other services, but

> that was an epic fail! Because apparently we use a boatload of data and you get a certain amount of data per month … at normal speed and after that [the providers] slow you down. And it is [via] satellite, so if there's bad weather you lose the service.

The family is continually evaluating its access needs and weighing concerns about data usage, weather conditions, and signal strength against the costs of available service options. Despite these struggles with access, Connie has some interesting thoughts about digital technology and rural populations.

During her interview she asks, "Don't you think kind of that technology is like the great equalizer between rural people and city people?" She continues, "It's probably not for everybody but certainly, people in a rural setting have access now to what they never would have unless they made a trip to a particular place." To follow-up, when asked if she thought people in her community were employing the access available in this way she replies, "I doubt it ... But as long as you have access to a computer and to the Internet, then you have access to everything that anybody, no matter where they live, has access to. That's kind of a cool thing."

Patricia Poe is a 44 year-old, white, married mother of two. Ragland, AL, is her hometown, and she has lived there all of her life. This is also her husband's hometown, so the family is deeply rooted in this community. Describing the town Patricia says, "It has always been rural. I don't think anything's going to change that, it's going to stay the same. And that's what I define rural as ... It's not going to change." Though this may seem like a negative assessment, Patricia notes she and her family choose to live in a rural setting. She is employed both as director of the town's small, public library and head librarian of the county library in a nearby town.

Not surprisingly, reading is an important part of Patricia's life. She spends twenty to thirty hours per week reading, mostly for entertainment. She says, "Reading, to me, is the best outlet. When I cannot express my feelings, I like to get in a book and read." Patricia remembers her parents and grandmother reading at home as she grew up. Yet, for Patricia, writing was more enjoyable at first than reading. She recalls writing for her elementary school teachers and keeping her own diaries as well. She says, "I really didn't get hooked on reading until I was I guess about twelve or thirteen ... I found Silhouette Special Edition for Teenagers ... I could still read those books today!" Interestingly, as Patricia's interest in reading sparked as a young teen, her interest in writing waned. She attributes this to an increase in the amount of writing assigned in her junior high years saying, "[W]e had seven classes, and tons of homework ... I just didn't like it anymore."

Despite her teenage loss of interest in writing, Patricia revealed in our discussion that writing is an important part of her everyday literacy practices. She spends ten to twenty hours each week engaged in writing activities mostly associated with her job. She composes reports for both the town council and the county library system on a regular basis. She also regularly posts on the library's Facebook page and keeps track of her to-do lists via OneNote. Recently, her husband began online college courses and she has helped edit and transcribe his papers. Of assisting with her husband's coursework Patricia says, "We were learning together. I had forgotten how to use a semicolon and [other] stuff, so I had to relearn ... this past year I have written a lot, more than I wanted to."

Growing up during the early stages of the technological revolution, Patricia's initial experiences with technology were in a high school vocational education class, though she admits she received no formal instruction then. She remembers, "At the time when we were in eleventh grade there were seniors there, and they already knew how to use [a computer]. So, they would just show us what to do ... we just taught ourselves basically." After high school Patricia did not use a computer again until she and her husband bought their first home computer in the late-1990s. Of that first computer she says, "It sat in our living room ... And [her oldest son] would play games, and I started off playing games, too ... It was 1998 when we finally got the Internet ... And that was fun, being on the Internet and finding out things." Patricia says that while she used the computer occasionally over the years for news and entertainment, it was not until she was hired as town librarian in 2003 that she came to use technology on a daily basis.

Today Patricia uses technology extensively. However, when she was hired she did not know how to use most of the technology associated with her job. Her oldest son, now twenty-seven, played a unique role as his mother's technological literacy sponsor. Patricia remembers, "He taught me how to use [the library's technology] because he had been going to the library and he knew the previous librarian. My director did not get to come for a couple weeks to teach me. So he taught me." Since then, she has mastered the technology necessary for her job. She regularly uses social media and the Internet to research titles, promote library events, and support literacy (digital and otherwise) within the community. In addition to these functional and rhetorical digital literacy practices, Patricia has purposefully developed her own critical digital literacy skills over the years saying, "It has taken me years to figure out [what to believe] and a lot of the emails that are going around, they just go to spam or trash."

In her role as librarian and community literacy sponsor, Patricia is in a position to observe and participate in the literacy practices of the library's patrons. She is familiar with the reading preferences of her regular patrons, and she frequently recommends books and Internet sources to fit patrons' needs and interests. And yet, while she feels confident in her role as literacy sponsor, she expresses some concern about the boundaries of the *digital* literacy sponsor, noting, "Some of my patrons, I want to say to them, 'Look, don't believe that email.' But I also don't want to tell them what to do." Patricia negotiates this boundary issue by only offering instruction or advice when a patron asks directly.

As a librarian, Patricia also possesses a unique perspective on access and the digital divide within her community. When asked if she thought a large percentage of her patrons used the library to obtain digital access she replies, "No, actually it's just the opposite. My [largest] percentages are the ones that read." She also reports that computer usage in the library is seasonal, saying that usage increases in the spring with students working on research papers. One exception to this pattern, Patricia notes, came three years ago after a devastating tornado hit the town. The library building and much of its contents was destroyed and the library was relocated to a temporary location while a new library was constructed. During this time Patricia noticed that the library played a larger role in providing digital connectivity and access to the community saying,

> We had more people that could not afford to have [access]. They may have had a computer at home, but they could not afford a printer, or they could not afford the Internet. So they would come to the library. Then there was the group of people taking classes online and many could not afford computers at all.

Patricia and her family definitely live a connected existence as they use digital devices around 50 hours per week. Though she acknowledges that technology is "an everyday thing; you have to have it nowadays," Patricia prefers printed material over digital for reading, saying, "I will always love a book in my hands ... with the written word in my hands I can escape better than I can with an E-reader." Still, her attitude about technology is positive as she concludes, "You have to have it. It's not gonna go away, so you might as well embrace it and learn how to use it."

Rhonda Lang is a 40 year-old, African-American, married, mother of two boys. Rhonda and her family live in the rural southwest Alabama town of Jackson, a community of roughly 5,000 residents. Rhonda has always lived in Jackson, and while she loves her hometown and believes it to be "a great place," she says that "it's a really good place for retirement ... 'Cause they've taken away a lot of the activities for the kids, and [kids] have to travel outside, like to Mobile or farther to have entertainment because nothing is here. So it's really kind of quiet." When asked about her early literacy experiences, she replied, "I really don't remember any of my childhood as far as, like, school reading. Well, I used to read at home. When my mama used to do hair, I used to get little books and read while she would do hair. 'Cause I didn't have nothing else to do." Rhonda related that her mother firmly believed in engaging in literacy-based activities, saying, "She was strict on all us with that. 'Cause she always told us she wanted us to do something in life besides just, you know, just not know nothing. So people wouldn't take advantage of you." Growing up, Rhonda has no memory of going to a computer lab in school, mainly because the school did not have computers available to for students to use, saying, "We didn't have that ... I don't remember having that. I really don't. But now, [the school's] got it, and [the students] know more than me. [Students] show me stuff and I be like—'Wow! I didn't know this.' But [the schools are] really moving on up." Rhonda credits enhanced access and the proliferation of computers for enabling today's students to be more digitally literate than she is even today, yet her abilities grow every day. She uses computers and mobile technologies for reading and writing, which continue to play profound roles in her life.

Rhonda's extracurricular literate practices are grounded in her faith, as she writes poetry and produces documents for church: "I love writing ... I write poems now ... I got, like, fifty something poems written already, [and] I do a lot of quick stuff in church. You know, if somebody need a reading or something really quick, I can write a poem within five minutes…they can be next on a program and I can just write them a quick poem and they read it." In her free time, she reads two to three hours per day from the Bible online and commentaries related to specific Bible verses or stories. A self-described "jack of all trades," Rhonda works as the technology coordinator at the public library in her town. She attended college for a short time to be a nurse, and says she had few meaningful experiences with technology and no training before accepting her current position out of necessity: "[The library] had a position open. And at that point I didn't have a job, and so I asked were they hiring and they said, 'Yeah, do you know anything about computers?' And I said, 'Yeah, a little.' ... I didn't know as much as I know now. When I first got this job I didn't know a whole lot, but as time progressed I learned more and more." She has developed her technological literacy on her own, through sponsoring library patrons in digital literacy, in the adult computer classes she teaches, and through networking with her co-workers. In her adult computer classes, she teaches 30 people per year, on average, to use computers for various tasks, including how to use e-mail and Microsoft Word and how to conduct research online.

As the technology coordinator for the library, Rhonda sponsors patrons regularly to become functional users of technology, and though she thinks critically about the information she finds online, she often faces ethical dilemmas when helping patrons find information: "Sometimes [patrons] come in and want to look up stuff that isn't … well, there's this man who come in and wants payday loans … loans here, loans there. He always lookin' for loans and I look it up 'cause it's my job, and I wanna say, 'Hey, you don't need to be gettin' these loans,' but I don't say nothing." Rhonda also worries about paying bills online and about hackers getting access to her email account and other personal information, saying, "People can go in and steal your identity and hack your pages and your phone numbers and they'll send you links to your phone and if you click on it they got access to everything about your phone and your computer. So basically ain't none of it's safe from hackers." Rhonda employs a skeptical approach to all of her Internet activities in order to balance her fears, and she teaches her adult computer students how to use technology as safely as they can by instructing them not to give out personal information and to also be wary of potential online risks. In her position at the library, she is a community literacy advocate and sponsor. Rhonda continues to learn new software and technologies, and she hopes to one day be a master of PowerPoint so that she may better serve the library's school-aged patrons.

Rhonda's family circumvents having Internet service at home through their use of mobile technology: "I just use my phone. We use the hotspot. We used to have Internet, you know, we used to pay for it. But it was like, 'Why?' when we got it right here on the phone. That's just extra money." When asked if she felt limited by the amount of data on her phone plan, she replied that she and her husband share data and have separate phone accounts, saying, "I use my phone one minute, you know, and then [my husband] use his phone … So we kinda share it that way. So you won't use all my data. You know, you use yours some." Rhonda also explained that while her family owns a computer for her sons to do homework, mainly, she uses her mobile devices when she is not at work: "If I need anything I use my phone … Cause I mean, it pulls up just about everything I need. I don't have no problem." In this way, cellular connectivity is working not only to bring faster and more reliable access to rural people but also to provide a more affordable way to access the Internet.

Kristy Randle, 43, is a white, married mother of one, and a returning college student who obtained her degree in English and journalism in spring 2014. Kristy was born in Charleston, South Carolina, but has lived all over the United States, and overseas, as the child of a military parent. Despite her mobility, however, she identifies strongly as a rural person and has strong roots in Springville, Alabama, a community near Birmingham. As Kristy puts it, "I identify [the town] … closely with home. The smell is home, the feeling, the people." Kristy defines "rural" in both negative and positive ways. On one hand, it represents a gap or absence of certain things: "few if any chain restaurants or stores. [On] the outskirts of the towns they lack modern conveniences like cable T.V. or city utilities." On the other hand, *rurality* represents things that Kristy values, such as a sense of connection and lifelong friendships, both for her and for her teenage son. During her adult lifetime, Kristy has had many roles, including beauty pageant contestant, salesperson, photographer, bakery and restaurant manager, stay-at-home mom, and full-time student. After graduating from high school, Kristy began taking classes at community college, but left school in order to get married and start her family. Years later, divorced, remarried, and back in the workforce, Kristy went back to college here at the University of Alabama, where she and her husband both decided to finish their degrees. For a time they commuted to school from their home in Springville, but the drive of almost two hours each way became unmanageable. In order to save money, they decided to buy a boat and live at a marina near their university. They return to their home in Springville for weekends and breaks.

Both literacy and digital literacy have been important aspects of Kristy's life. As a returning college student, she spends 20-25 hours a week reading or writing. But she notes that writing was important to her even before she went back to school: "I journaled like nobody's business!" She kept notebooks during her pregnancy and tried her hand at writing a romance novel, saying, " I still have the laptop that has [the work] on it. One day I might go back, but I'm kind of scared at the same time. My writing back then.. it's not at the same level as it is now. My writing is neater now, there's a purpose." Kristy explains that when she returned to college she was scared about the expectations for writing in her advanced English classes, and she describes her first attempt to write a long paper as an "epic fail" (though she didn't literally fail). With dedication on Kristy's part, and the help of a few professors who worked with her outside of class, she gradually began to produce longer and more successful academic papers.

Born in the early 70s, Kristy has witnessed the rise of the personal computer, the advent of the Internet, the digital revolution, and the emergence of Web 2.0. Though many of her daily activities are mediated through technology, she has clear memories of a time when that was not the case. Kristy remembers the advent of the electronic typewriter and the transition to word processing. She remembers having a Commodore 64 computer at home, and later on, learning to use computers on Macintosh machines in high school. Part of her education included a class where she learned to write basic computer code. Describing this class, Kristy says

> Our assignment was, we had to write this program to calculate grades. So one of us would do it, and each of us would get the disk passed down and we would do through and copy it and make a few changes just to get it done. [This was 1987] and we had this attitude, "what the hell are we going to use this for?"

However, Kristy's real introduction to computers came in her professional life when she got a job at a department store that sold computers in its electronic department. Then, as she puts it, the birth of the Internet and the arrival of e-mail allowed her to connect with family members and friends, and she gradually became more wired as the technology evolved: "I was e-mailing my mom ... e-mailing different friends who had moved off ... e-mailing those folks that were states away ... I didn't use the computer every single day, like I do now. I mean it's a night and day transition to what I am now. It just kind of evolved."

By her own description, Kristy is a highly connected user of technology. She estimates spending 4 hours a day using her laptop or computer for schoolwork, 5 hours a day using a tablet device, and keeping her smartphone at hand in addition to these other devices, for about 8-10 hours of the day. She uses these devices for word processing, social media, e-mail, gaming, voice/texting, photo editing, and web browsing, among other things. Digital technologies and digital literacies serve various purposes for her. They have been essential to her academic work and her training as a student journalist. In her interview, Kristy describes how she uses social media to report on local politics: "If I need to do a follow up question with [a state representative], well, we've become friends on Facebook. I did an interview with him the other day. And with somebody like that, I didn't want to misquote him, especially when doing a controversial topic. So I Facebooked him and I said, 'Look, I know you're in session, I'm writing up your article now, and I couldn't understand it on the tape, and I really want to make sure I have this quote.'" Similarly, she uses Twitter to send questions to state politicians. As she puts it, "You can pose a question to them, 'Now what was this bill for?' You gotta be informed, like on say [Alabama] House Bill 56 and criminal expungement ... 'Have there been any changes in senate judiciary on House Bill 56 since it's being re-debated?' You can ask them that question as a journalist [and] get a quote on Twitter." Digital technologies also serve very practical purposes for Kristy because sometimes her WIFI service on the boat is more reliable than her wireless phone service. She notes that her family members use Facebook to send urgent messages because it's more reliable than calling or texting.

In terms of her access to digital technologies and the digital divide, however, Kristy notes that "in rural areas, it's more constricted. We have one phone carrier for the entire town. We did not have dial-up until about four years ago. And I didn't realize how slow it was until we got high speed. So that's your limitation. If you're in the town of Springville, you have a little bit more choice because the cable company carries Internet. Where I live, I'm on the outskirts, so I don't get cable." For Kristy, technology, has been essential in helping her bridge the distance between her rural community and her temporary home on the boat.

Kody Thomas is a 31 year-old, white, college graduate, part-time tutor, aspiring writer, and homeschooling mother of three. Originally from Eutaw, Alabama, she grew up in a small town in Mississippi, and now lives in Reform, AL. When asked to describe her small town, Kody says, "We have a whopping TWO red lights ... which is kind of a big deal for Pickens county. This is one of those communities where everybody knows your business, your family, your history, etc. Which of course has its downsides, but can also be a good thing." While she has worked and attended college in an urban area, she prefers "to commute rather than live in the city. [She] simply does not like being stuck in a crush of that many people all of the time; it feels too unnatural to [her]." Kody is an avid reader and writer who was always a good student. She went to a well-respected public boarding school for high school and then attended college for three semesters before leaving school to get married and start her family. During the years that she was out of school, she did procurement work for a trucking company and became proficient in creating spreadsheets and using Excel. Seven years later, she went back to school to finish her degree.

Kody is both highly literate and very connected to the digital world. She estimates that she spends close to forty hours a week reading and twelve to fourteen hours a week writing. She reads and writes in diverse ways, from the mundane activities of using social networks or writing lists, to reading literary and popular fiction, and writing prose. Her mom, who was an avid reader, shaped her literacy practices in significant ways. Kody has vivid memories of going on road trips with her mom when she was a kid. They would drive from their small town to a larger city where her mom could buy books: "she would buy a new book at the bookstore every month and would read it while driving home. The book on the steering wheel, I am not lying ... And she was a hobbyist writer ... seven years ago she passed away, and I'm still finding manuscripts that she had written on an old school typewriter." During her school years, Kody frequently read material far above her grade level. As a reader, she enjoys both literary and popular fiction; She is proud of a college paper she wrote comparing the *Twilight* series to *Paradise Lost* (it earned an A-). Although she is a successful, and prolific writer, Kody is also very self-critical. She has kept diaries through the years, but destroyed most of them. As she puts it, "I hate my own writing. I will write something, and, a year later, I'll go back through and read it. If it's worth saving, I'll leave it be, but if I think it's crap, I'll just delete."

Kody was in the eighth grade when she first got access to computers at school. She learned basic word processing skills, such as using Clip Art and making tables, but because the technology was new to the teachers as well, they were learning it along with the students. Access was limited at that time, because the school had only twelve computers to serve all four hundred students. In high school, Kody first got access to the Internet. The use of the technology was not immediately apparent; students used it to send email to one another, but since they were at boarding school, Kody says, e-mail was "nothing we couldn't have done by walking down the hallway and knocking on a door." Later, Kody used the school library for Internet research, and began to type instead of handwrite her school papers.

In the late 90s, around the time that many Americans were becoming connected to the Internet and personal computer use was increasing throughout the nation, Kody, too, became a more regular computer user. She got her first home computer when her boyfriend at the time helped her to build one: "He had a bunch of spare parts, because he was [a] technophile. He had a box of spare parts. So we took a tower and found a hard drive that worked and went digging through and we found power strips and some memory and a motherboard. We threw it all together and started wiggling wires and pushing things into place until it powered up and worked." She used that computer to play games and for dial-up Internet access. Kody describes how she acquired her next computer after this one. This computer was reduced for clearance after another customer had purchased and returned it: "It didn't work, and knowing it didn't work, I bought it. I was able to send it off and get the warranty to fix it, which was why I bought it. And it was $350, maybe $400, somewhere in that range. But the same ones like it that were new were $900-$1200."

Kody is an avid reader, writer, and user of technology. In fact, it seems difficult to sort out her "digital" reading and writing from her "traditional" literacy because she does so much of both. As previously mentioned, she estimates that she spends forty hours a week on reading and writing texts that include "literature, news, humor, brain candy, romance novels, and sometimes help wanted and circular ads." The scope of her literary reading ranges from Harlequin romances to Shakespearean comedies. She does much of her reading on her phone, using sites that include Al.com, Yahoo News, and Google News. For books, however, she prefers to use the actual texts rather than e-readers. Before Kody purchased a tablet, she had some reservations about e-readers: "So many people are realizing that when you purchase [an electronic] book, you're purchasing a right to look at the book. You don't actually own it, and they can take it from you. If I want to purchase it, I want it [she claps twice] right there."

The technologies she frequently uses include her iPhone, laptop, and Xbox. She uses Facebook to connect with other moms and Twitter to keep up with some of her interests (She notes that she likes to follow the Twitter feeds of literary figures such as Lord Voldemort and Jane Eyre). She often jots down notes for story ideas and hopes to use some of her life story as a basis for her work in the future. For Kody, digital literacy has been not only essential to her academic life but also important to her personal and domestic life, as it helps her to generate ideas and to pursue her interest in literature, to stay connected with other moms, and to homeschool her boys. Her children have used technology to do online lessons, to check out electronic library books to read on her tablet (purchased during the course of our study). They use an app that reads aloud to the children and highlights words and sentences, helping them begin to read independently.

Synthesis and Conclusion

Rurality

Because rurality is the central feature that shaped our participants' access to technology, we were interested in their perceptions of their communities and of the term itself: what does it mean to be rural? In the introduction to this piece, we note that "rural" is not a fixed label but a determination made for rhetorical, economic, and political purposes. In a similar way, "rural" does not have a shared definition for our participants, but rather, represents a range of factors. When asked to describe her community, Kody says that Reform, AL, is rural because only 1600 people live there and because the entire county (Pickens County) has fewer people in it than Northport, AL, the "sister city" of our university town. She suggests, only somewhat ironically, that her town must be rural because it only has two stoplights. Rhonda defines herself as "less rural" than many of her library patrons because she lives in town rather than in the country, and she has access to more conveniences (like better Internet service) than those who live farther out. As she puts it: "it's hard. You ain't gonna get Internet 'cause that's why most [library patrons] come here. That's the reason I consider not being rural myself. I know we *are*, but they're way out there, they have to come here 'cause they don't have any access." And Kristy considers herself rural even though she has spent a good portion of her life in urban areas. Our interviews suggest that "rurality" can be considered a spectrum. Moreover, while our participants sometimes define rurality in terms of the things that are lacking—stores, or easy Internet access, for instance—they are quick to point out the positive aspects of rural life, including a sense of connectedness and belonging, a feeling of safety and friendliness, and a slower-paced style of life.

Sponsorship and Digital Literacy

In her landmark article, "Sponsors of Literacy," Deborah Brandt argues that we can better understand the development of literacy in its social, political, and economic contexts by tracing the relationships between learners and the individuals who have sponsored them. Literacy sponsors, writes Brandt, are:

> … agents, local or distant, concrete or abstract, who enable, support, teach, model, as well as recruit, regulate, suppress, or withhold literacy-and gain advantage by it in some way. Just as the ages of radio and television accustom us to having programs brought to us by various commercial sponsors, it is useful to think about who or what underwrites occasions of literacy learning and use. (166)

As librarians, two of our participants serve as sponsors of digital literacy in their day-to-day, professional lives. For Rhonda, sponsoring others is an important source of pride:

> When [I started] teaching computer class, I had a lot of people that saw me in town and they'd say, 'If it wasn't for you I would never have learned computers … I didn't even know how to turn it on, and now I know how to get on there, check my e-mail, navigate, see what I need'. … if you calculate fifteen people over seven/eight years, you've touched a lot of people lives, and they will remind you.

In exploring how our participants were sponsored by others, and in turn sponsored other learners, we began to think about how individuals become sponsors. What qualifies someone as a sponsor of digital literacy? For our participants, the role of digital literacy sponsor was not limited to those with a high level of computer proficiency. More so than technological "capital," our interviews suggest, digital sponsorship is often a natural result of a willingness to learn. In this sense, it seems different from traditional sponsorship. In order to teach others to read, in other words, we would normally need to know at least a little bit more than they do. With technology, our participants often described themselves as learning *with* others, as well as through their own resourcefulness. Patricia, for instance, did not know how to use computers to check out books when she first got her job at the library, but her son, a regular patron who encouraged her to apply for the job, showed her how. When it comes to using technology in school, several of our participants mentioned that technologies such as word processing were so unfamiliar when they were first introduced, that teachers and students had to learn them together. "We just taught ourselves," as Patricia put it, or, as Kody says, "the teacher was learning as she was teaching us, because she had been using a typewriter."

In her interview with Allen, Rhonda describes how she became a technology coordinator before she had acquired the skills she would need in this position:

> I had to teach the students so I had to teach myself first: to look up stuff on the Internet, to navigate and see what I could come up with, and to do programs. Microsoft Word—the fonts, the styles ... Powerpoint ... I didn't know nothing about any of that until I started here. And that's when I started and I learned it.

She notes that she still continues to learn in her current position: "I've learned a little about Excel. Just a little. I ain't quite got it yet, but I got the book." When our participants learn to use new technologies from their children, on their own, or with their schoolteachers, they "flip the script" of traditional sponsorship, whereby the person with the most status is usually the one assumed to know best.

Economies, Resourcefulness, Access

In thinking about our participants' experiences in relation to the economic and political issues surrounding the digital divide, an interesting paradox emerges. On one hand, all of our participants acknowledge that they have struggled at times to get reliable access to the Internet, and that their communities are less connected than the nearest urban centers. On the other hand, their responses do not dwell on that gap; rather, they tend to emphasize their sense of connectivity, and the strategies that they personally use to bridge the divide. Throughout our interviews, we were struck by our participants' resourcefulness—in gaining Internet access, in learning to use new devices in new contexts, and in acquiring technological devices that fit within their family budgets. Kody, for instance, describes many of the strategies she has used to acquire computers at an affordable price—whether by having a computer built for her, or by using the warranty program that came with a computer returned by another customer. Likewise, Connie explains how after years of buying popular brands, she learned to compare machine specifications among brands to find an affordable computer that met her family's needs. These examples illustrate Selfe and Hawisher's point that individuals "exert their own powerful agency," not only in using, but in acquiring technologies.

Moreover, economies of access played a large role in determining how and to what extent our participants were able to use technologies for reading and writing. Scholarship on digital literacy has tended to neglect such mundane details as the ways individuals get access, the options for access in particular locations, and the financial expense that access incurs (Selfe and Hawisher, Grabill). These details may seem to be matters or luck or personal choice, but in fact, we argue, when it comes to digital literacy, the mundane details are quite profound. Throughout our discussions we found that cost and service provider options were major factors in our participants' levels and quality of access. Connie talks at length about her family's ongoing struggle to gain affordable, reliable access. She notes that with only one local telephone company, her options for Internet service are "very limited." Through the years the family has tried several providers, including the local phone company and a few satellite-based services. She explains that her family is continually evaluating their need for access and weighing concerns about data usage, weather conditions, and signal strength against the costs. Bad weather can make some providers unreliable, some providers' signals do not reach throughout the entire house, and other providers' connectivity speeds decrease dramatically once the data limit is reached—the family must consider these points regularly.

Like Connie, Rhonda has tried several strategies in order to gain reliable, affordable access. Though she lives in an area where wired access is available, she and her husband use their smartphones as wireless hotspots. They take turns using each other's phones to avoid data overages. Rhonda says this option is less expensive, though they still struggle at times with slow connection speed. Connie speculated in her interview that technology might be a "great equalizer," for rural people. It indeed may be, but only for those who can afford reliable, consistent access.

Kinds of Literacy/Contexts for Literacy

Our participants use digital literacy in a variety of contexts—personal, spiritual, academic, domestic, and professional. They display a range of literacy abilities—functional, critical, and rhetorical—in these many contexts. All of our interviewees have a high level of functional literacy, as they use basic technologies on a daily basis. But we would argue that the definition of functional digital literacy might be better understood if we include in it the ability to find solutions for access. Our participants display this practical know-how when they create internet hotspots or share their phones with family members to avoid overage fees.

Likewise, critical literacy comes in different forms, including the ability to question information that participants encounter online (as Patricia, Connie, and Rhonda discuss in excerpts above), to use technology to become politically engaged (Kristy) and to make decisions about pedagogy for homeschooling mothers (Connie, Kody). For those who are in a position of literacy *sponsor*, a concern with critical literacy sometimes forces them to negotiate the boundaries of that sponsorship. The librarians, for instance, wrestle with the question of whether to warn patrons about the Internet scams they encounter when they access e-mail on library computers. Our participants also demonstrate a sense of critical literacy when they describe how they consult web sources in order to verify the accuracy of information they find online (Rhonda, Patricia, and Connie). As Connie put it, "If you can get three places that say the same thing then you're fairly certain." Critical literacy also means being aware of the economies of reading and writing online. Kody, in particular, expresses reservations about e-books because she is aware that when downloading books, individual consumers don't really "own" those books in the same way that we can own a physical book that we purchase at a bookstore.

Conclusion

With increasing interest in digital and online instruction at all levels of education, along with an increasing use of the Internet for e-commerce as well as to maintain personal/professional connections, digital literacy has never been so important. Yet for many Americans, owning a computer and having reliable access remain difficult hurdles to overcome. We, as researchers, acknowledge that technology evolves at a pace faster than qualitative research can match. Nonetheless, we hope that research like ours will bring human voices to the abundance of data on digital usage and access, an element often neglected in statistical measurements.

Digital literacy plays many different roles in the lives of our participants—from being a shared activity with family members (as in reading with children, playing video games together, or helping one another with school work), to being an important part of their professional and spiritual lives. Literacy is a legacy that family members pass down from one generation to the next, as with Kody and her memories of her mom driving home with a book on the steering wheel. Each participant marks the passing of time through technological advancements, as they are able to recall each "era" of their lives by the life spans of the technologies that emerged during these "eras." Further, technology is so ubiquitous that we all forget how profoundly important it is and how much the technologies used for reading and writing have changed in the span of one generation.

One of the most profound changes is the increasing reliance on mobile devices—especially smartphones. Undoubtedly, the use of "smart" devices will have a dramatic effect on everyday literacy practices in the generations to come, and mobile technologies will play an important role in overcoming the gap created by the digital divide. We hope that our research clarifies that while mobile technology has become more widely available, adequate digital access still depends on factors like location, cost, and infrastructure. We encourage future researchers to look more closely at how rural Americans are using their mobile devices to read and write, search for and evaluate information, produce texts, and narrow the gap caused by the digital divide.

Endnotes

1. We thank our undergraduate research assistant, Taylor Sheeran, who assisted with interview transcription and with coding the data.

2. We modified Hawisher and Selfe's questionnaire by limiting it to questions that were most germane to our focus, and by dividing it into a background portion and an interview protocol. We realize that it is not possible to draw general conclusions about rural people, both because of our small sample size and the qualitative nature of the project, but also because "rural" is a complex term used to describe a variety of people with distance from urban areas as their common link.

Works Cited

Besser, Howard. "The Next Digital Divides." *Teaching to Change L.A.* 1.2 (2001). Web. 15 April 2012.
Brandt, Deborah. *Literacy in American Lives.* New York: Cambridge UP, 2001. Print.
_____. "Sponsors of Literacy." *College Composition and Communication* 49.2 (1998): 165-85. Web. 8 July 2013.
Bucholtz, Shawn. "Defining the 'Rural' in Rural America." *Amber Waves* 6:3 (2008): 8-34. Web. 9 August 2012.
"ConnectEd: President Obama's Plan for Connecting All Schools to the Digital Age." Whitehouse.gov. ConnectEd Initiative, 2013. PDF. 3 March 2014.
Donehower, Kim, Charlotte Hogg, and Eileen E. Schell. *Rural Literacies.* Carbondale: Southern Illinois UP, 2007. Print.
Fox, Susannah and Lee Rainie. "The Web at 25 in the U.S." PewInternet.org. Pew Research Center, 2014. Web. 10 May 2014.
Grabill, Jeffrey T. "On Divides and Interfaces: Access, Class, and Computers." *Computers and Composition* 20.4 (2003): 455-72. Web. 3 March 2014.
Hawisher, Gail E., Cynthia L. Selfe, Brittney Moraski, and Melissa Pearson. "Becoming Literate in the Information Age: Cultural Ecologies and the Literacies of Technology." *College Composition and Communication* 55:4 (2004): 642-92. Web. 10 May 2014.
Housing Assistance Council. "What is 'Rural'?." *Rural Voices* 18:1 (2012): 8-10. Web. 3 March 2014.
Royster, Jacqueline Jones and Gesa E. Kirsch. *Feminist Rhetorical Practices: New Horizons for Rhetoric, Composition, and Literacy Studies.* Carbondale: Southern Illinois UP, 2012. Print.

Ruecker, Todd. "Exploring the Digital Divide on the U.S.-Mexico Border Through Literacy Narratives." *Computers and Composition* 29.3 (2012): 239-53. Web. 10 May 2014.

Selber, Stuart A. *Multiliteracies for a Digital Age*. Carbondale: Southern Illinois UP, 2004. Print.

Selfe, Cynthia and Gail E. Hawisher. *Literate Lives in the Information Age: Narratives of Literacy from the United States*. Mahwah: Lawrence Erlbaum Associates, 2004. Print.

Severson, Kim. "Digital Age is Slow to Arrive in Rural America." *New York Times*, 11 Feb 2011. Web. 14 April 2011.

Author Bios

Jennie Vaughn is a PhD candidate in the CRES (Composition, Rhetoric, and English Studies) program at the University of Alabama. She is currently writing her dissertation, a feminist historiography about cookbooks written by Alabama women from 1850-1930. She also teaches undergraduate writing courses including composition technical writing, and professional writing.

Allen Harrell earned his M.A. in CRES (Composition, Rhetoric, and English Studies) at the University of Alabama. He teaches freshman composition courses as an adjunct at Alabama Southern Community College. Allen's research interests include digital literacy, rurality, politics of identity and place, rural student attrition, and the politics and rhetoric of Christian culture.

Amy E. Dayton is associate professor of English at University of Alabama, where she teaches advanced writing and graduates courses in literacy and composition theory and pedagogy. Her research interests include historiography, community literacy, and teacher training. Her collection, *Assessing the Teaching of Writing: Twenty-First Century Trends and Technologies*, is forthcoming from Utah State University Press.

Transformative Learning, Affect, and Reciprocal Care in Community Engagement

Ashley J. Holmes

Drawing on interviews with writing teachers, this article highlights some of the affective responses that may arise for students, community partners, and teachers when we situate our pedagogies in public sites beyond the classroom. I analyze a teacher-narrated moment of student distress to demonstrate how theories of transformative learning might help us productively theorize affect in service-learning and community-based education. To conclude, I offer a reciprocal model of care that employs tenets of feminist pedagogy, such as transparency and decentering of authority, and that acknowledges the valid emotions students, teachers, and community members may experience. I call for community literacy practitioners to see the power of all participants to both give and receive care in transformative education.

Keywords: tranformative learning; community engagement; care; reciprocity; service learning; feminist pedagogy

Introduction

Service learning and community engagement have gained prominence as pedagogical approaches that can lead to deeply impactful, even transformative, learning experiences for students. However, when we open our pedagogies to a more expansive public through community engagement, any safety that a classroom could provide may be entirely absent. Partnering with the local community can be risky, disorienting, and emotionally demanding for students and teachers. Yet these risks also offer the potential for rewards, and many advocates of community engagement value these pedagogies precisely because of the personal growth and profound learning students may experience. Those of us who incorporate service and community-based learning into our courses often hope to expose students to diverse populations, prompt them to confront "real world" problems in their community, and offer a reflective classroom space for students to work through the dissonance that may accompany these experiences.[1] However, more recently, I have begun questioning the affective components of community-based projects and whether, as a teacher who strives to approach students as whole learners, I am fully prepared to embrace the emotions that may arise for students in my courses.

I first began questioning the role of affect in community engagement pedagogies when I interviewed writing teachers as part of a multi-institutional, comparative study of going public with composition pedagogy (see Holmes, "Public Pedagogy").[2] A number of the teachers who participated in my study explained how they use service learning as one way for students to both learn from and contribute to the local community. Overwhelmingly, these teachers noted their commitment to community outreach because of its positive impact on student engagement and learning. However, paired with the praise were comments that indicated teachers' awareness of the potential risks and emotional demands of incorporating community-based projects, particularly ones that involve venturing beyond the classroom and/or situating student writing within increasingly public contexts.

The narratives teachers shared, some of which I analyze in the coming pages, raised questions for me about how practitioners of community engagement pedagogies should respond to affective reactions. As much as I value the way service learning can be productively disruptive or unsettling, I also question a pedagogy that purposefully exposes students to emotionally-demanding scenarios without providing the kind of support to help them make sense of their experiences and move toward learning. In spring 2014, debates about the values and risks of purposefully exposing college students to challenging and emotionally-demanding course content arose in response to moves on several campuses to institute "trigger warnings" on syllabi (Medina). Commonly used on feminist blogs, though also used in other feminist and non-feminist spaces, trigger warnings are meant to caution readers/viewers about graphic or explicit content—e.g., rape, abuse, torture—that may be upsetting and which may trigger a flashback for someone who has experienced trauma. While proponents argue that using trigger warnings in higher education would protect students, many faculty opponents counter that supporting such alerts "suggest[s] a fragility of mind that higher learning is meant to challenge, not embrace" (Medina); in other words, many teachers believe that an important part of learning in college means discussing and experiencing texts and issues that may be out of students' comfort zones. While the trigger warning debates did not explicitly interrogate the role of service learning as a potential trigger, I think many community literacy practitioners would agree that students participating in such programs often encounter scenarios or interactions that could be upsetting. Indeed, such moments of discomfort can be transformative for students' learning, echoing what opponents of trigger warnings have contended. However, as proponents of trigger warnings continue to question, how much discomfort is too much?

In an effort to find an approach to community engagement that addressed some of my concerns, I turned to feminist scholarship, which I believe provides a frame through which we can problematize disorientation and theorize a reciprocal approach to care. In the following pages, I highlight some of the emotional risks that may arise for students, community partners, and teachers when we situate our pedagogies in public sites beyond the university. I suggest how theories of transformative learning might help teachers and community partners productively theorize affective dimensions of learning in community engagement. Using an example from one of the teachers in my study, I analyze a moment of emotional distress a student experienced resulting from the service-learning component of her business writing course. Reflecting on the role of affect for students, teachers, and community partners in service learning, I contend that the example should cause community literacy practitioners to pause and contemplate our responsibilities to each other in community-based projects. I conclude by suggesting a reciprocal model of care that draws on the strengths of a feminist standpoint while discarding the traditional, gender-specific positioning of care and nurturance as women's work. I argue that by employing transparency and decentering authority, we open opportunities to acknowledge and validate the emotions that students, teachers, and community members may experience through a transformative, community-based education. I situate transparency and decentering authority within the lens of a well-known tenet in community literacy scholarship: reciprocity; I call for community literacy practitioners to see the power of all participants to both give and receive care in transformative education.

Risks & Rewards of Community Engagement

Teachers who choose to employ community literacy, service learning, or other kinds of community-based projects do so for a number of reasons, ranging from improving one's local community to helping instill in students a sense of civic responsibility to putting course content into action. However, the foundation of the choice—whether or not to include community engagement in one's course—is primarily pedagogical; we choose to engage students in community-based work because we believe it is valuable for their learning. For community literacy practitioners, situating student experience, learning, and writing in public sites beyond the classroom provides a meaningful context through which to explore social issues while facilitating student learning. The rewards of higher levels of engagement, transfer of knowledge, and potential transformation are certainly attractive, but do they outweigh the risks of situating one's pedagogy in the often messy unknowns of public communities beyond the classroom?

In the interviews I conducted for my study, writing teachers repeatedly noted that students became more engaged when the course design involved community-based and/or public writing projects. For example Jan Cooper, who co-teaches a field-based writing course at Oberlin College, noted that getting students out into the local community to conduct ecological labs in the river watershed and interview local farmers resulted in "a level of immediacy that engaged [students] more thoroughly" (Cooper). Similarly, Crystal Fodrey, who taught composition courses at the University of Arizona, asked students to analyze spaces that "exhibit inequalities of race, class, gender, sexuality, ability, etc.," and she found that prompting students to leave the classroom and enter local community spaces "woke [students] up" in ways that made them "more engaged" (Fodrey). High levels of engagement have an impact on how successfully students learn concepts. "Students must engage to learn," note Peter Felten and H-Dirksen L. Bauman, "and high quality institutions support frequent, deep engaged activities by students to promote learning" (367). In other words, higher levels of engagement can have a positive impact on students' learning.

Higher levels of student engagement can lead to the possibility of long-term transfer of core concepts from the course. Research on knowledge transfer notes that a learner may have a "life transforming experience" in which she or he "becom[es] someone ... new" (Tuomi-Gröhn and Engeström 27). When the transfer of knowledge is transformative, learners experience "changes in identity as well as knowledge and skill" (Tuomi-Gröhn and Engeström 28). A transformative education that alters students' worldview aligns with many of the social justice goals of community-based projects, such as challenging dominant ideologies, deconstructing hierarchies, and critiquing biases. The long-term benefit for students is a new frame of reference for understanding the world, and the benefit for teachers, community members, and society is moving one step closer towards an informed citizenry who asks critical questions and works to eradicate injustice.

When we partner with communities beyond the classroom, however, students are exposed to different kinds of risks that can be disorienting, even if they are ultimately productive for their learning. Community engagement projects pose a unique set of risks, in part because teachers have little control over what students may experience and how those experiences may clash with students' personal worldviews. The risks associated with community projects are part of what makes them attractive to many teachers, including myself, because such contexts prompt students to address issues that may not have come up within the relative safety of the classroom. Some research on knowledge transfer also suggests that risk taking can enhance learning and transfer; however, as David Guile and Michael Young note, "learners need to be supported" through processes of collaboration, discussion, and risk taking (74). How can teachers create a productive tension between risk and safety, and, at what point does risk-taking complicate the goals of learning and transfer in one's community-based pedagogy? Without risk, students may not have the opportunity to address tough issues or face dilemmas that would prompt a transformation in their worldview. However, without some degree of safety, support, and care, students may shut down—unable to deal with the overwhelming dissonances, let alone move towards any meaningful learning. As teachers trained in our disciplines, not in therapy, how can we acknowledge and give credence to students' valid emotions while still moving towards more meaningful learning? To begin answering these questions, I review scholarship on theories of transformative learning and education, as well as the role of affect and emotion in service learning and community literacy pedagogies.

Transformation & Affect in Community-Based Learning

Most teachers who enact community literacy projects are deeply engaged in transformative learning, but we do not always have the language for interpreting and theorizing this practice. I believe that transformative learning, as a theory coming out of education and curriculum studies, can be a valuable tool for community literacy practitioners to understand the potential disorientation and emotional responses that may accompany transformation in community-based education. In his theory of transformative learning developed in the early 1990s, Jack Mezirow describes a kind of conversion that can happen when adults wrestle with new information. Through what Mezirow calls "perspective transformation experiences," learners shift their assumptions to cope with and make sense of newly learned information. He defines transformative learning as "the process by which we transform our taken-for-granted frames of reference (meaning perspectives, habits of mind, mind-sets) to make them more inclusive, discriminating, open, emotionally capable of change, and reflective so that they may generate beliefs and opinions that will prove more true or justified to guide action" (Mezirow, *Learning as Transformation* 8). Transformation involves becoming self-reflective and critically aware of our assumptions and how they "constrain the way we perceive, understand and feel about our world"; as a result of this critical self-awareness, we open possibilities for a new perspective—one that may be more "inclusive, discriminating and integrative" (Mezirow *Transformative Dimensions* 168). Mezirow describes ten phases that learners may go through when experiencing transformation, beginning with (1) a disorienting dilemma and (2) self-examination with feelings of fear, anger, guilt, or shame (Mezirow, *Learning as Transformation*).[3] For this paper, I focus on these first two phases—rather than all ten—because they represent the root or spark of transformative learning, but also because they are the most explicitly emotional, drawing attention to the affective dimensions of teaching and learning.

Other education researchers and cognitive psychologists have theorized the disorientation that may accompany new knowledge, but these theories are much less attentive to the emotional components of transformation. For example, Leon Festinger theorizes "cognitive dissonance" as the condition during which one's existing set of beliefs, knowledge, or opinions are questioned and which leads to an activity meant to reduce the dissonance (3–4). Similarly, Jean Piaget theorized learning as an ongoing cycle of equilibration, with disequilibrium leading to equilibrium (7). Cognitive dissonance and disequilibrium are useful concepts, but because both lack attention to the role of affect, they connote a hyper-rational, masculinized approach to learning that serves to replicate divisions between cognition and emotion. In fact, the study of emotions in pedagogy has traditionally been under-theorized because of the unnecessary divides between cognition and affect, mind and body. Moreover, affect continues to be dismissed as "something dangerous, personal, irrelevant, and counter-productive" (DeGenaro 195). In his analysis of Lynn Worsham's seminal article, "Going Postal: Pedagogic Violence and the Schooling of Emotion," William DeGenaro highlights that even critical pedagogies, according to Worsham, "lack a useful understanding of affect and tend to reinforce a reason/mind-emotion/body binary" (195). While Mezirow's theory of transformative learning is certainly not a panacea for these deep-seated binaries, it perhaps offers community literacy practitioners a more nuanced, integrated approach to theorizing student learning because it implicates emotional considerations in the processes of making meaning.

A number of transformative learning theorists have identified the important role of emotions—such as loss, grief, and frustration—in the process of transformation. Sue M. Scott likens the process of transformation to letting something go: "an old way of seeing or doing is changed to a new way of seeing or doing. Something that is familiar must be denied" (41); such a loss can be upsetting and disorienting. Similarly, Sue L. T. McGregor found overlap between theories of transformative learning and stages of grief. McGregor analyzes student freewrites from an intensive, seven-day summer institute on consumerism and peace. Like Scott, McGregor ultimately realizes that what her students were experiencing was a sense of loss, what she identifies as "grief before growth" (51). The grief in students' writing represented feelings of being overwhelmed and powerless, as well as frustrated by their new perspectives. McGregor used the institute as a reflective, supportive space to help students move through their emotions with the goal of helping them arrive at a position of empowerment and agency.

Grief and other emotions can present barriers to learning, but they can also be necessary steps toward transformation. Barbara Schneider argues that we need to more fully explore affective barriers to learning; she looks at affect in terms of students' racist dispositions when confronting multicultural texts. Schneider employs Cornel West's conception of discernment, which "requires an examination of consciousness, a search for insight, [and] a self-reflexivity ... [in] affective as well as cognitive processes" (927). Schneider argues that teachers can use discernment in the classroom as a method of "schooling the emotions" to help students avoid habitually racist ways of reading and discussing difference (927). Through discernment students can gain empathy, taking on what West identifies as an "other-centered rather than self-centered" attitude—a change that mirrors the way Mezirow describes a transformed perspective or worldview (qtd. in Schneider 928). To initiate these changes in students' dispositions, teachers must shift their attention from the "rational or mechanical ... to the affective and attitudinal" (Schneider 928). Schneider's argument for the use of discernment to change students' attitudes and dispositions is quite similar to the use of critical self-reflection in order to transform one's perspective. Part of the significance of Schneider's contribution is how she directs our attention to the role of affect in this process; in short, attending to students' emotions is a necessary component for the deep learning that results in transformation.

In "Affective Dimensions of Service Learning," DeGenaro claims that affect and the role of emotions in the teaching of writing have garnered "much critical attention from compositionists writ large but little attention in the service learning literature" (192). Nonetheless, emotional responses continue to emerge in community literacy work. For example, Ellen Cushman and Erik Green note that an unexpected result of their work with the Cherokee Nation was the "very emotional response that we had with the material"; during the process of sharing research papers, they recall that one student "broke into tears" (187). Like DeGenaro, though, I believe that service learning and community literacy practitioners would benefit from a "more careful consideration of the affective affinities of both students and teachers," as well as community partners, "involved in the service learning enterprise" (192). Though DeGenaro does not employ transformative learning theory explicitly, many of his ideas align with how Mezirow has theorized perspective transformation; for example, DeGenaro contends that, as a result of service learning, "students and teachers both have the potential to have their respective world views changed" (197). DeGenaro describes affect in service learning as "initial felt senses"; his work highlights how an encounter with a homeless person at a food bank, for instance, results first and foremost in a sensation: "Before [students] begin to rationalize, analyze, critique, form a response, take action, or even just describe the experience, (all of which are cognitive activities we ask service learning students to do as part of their writing assignments), a sensation occurs, contributing to a potential to feel, act, think, and formulate verbal responses" (197). Like Mezirow's first phases of transformation—a disorienting dilemma and self-examination with a range of potential feelings—students in service learning courses may very well be disoriented the first time they encounter a homeless person, and they would certainly have initial felt senses resulting from that interaction. DeGenaro acknowledges the important role of affect in service learning experiences, especially because those experiences have the potential for being emotionally-demanding and potentially transformative.

Theories of transformation often distinguish between transformative learning and transformative education (Karpiak; Mezirow; McGregor). The former might be prompted by a life event, such as the loss of one's job or the death of a family member, whereas the latter involves a "planned for and facilitated" educational journey (McGregor 55). Transformative learning may happen as the result of transformative education, though not necessarily, and transformative learning can happen outside of educational contexts. However, movements toward self-reflection and transformation can be "significantly influenced by educational interventions" (Mezirow, *Transformative Dimensions* 161). I see choosing to implement service-learning and community engagement pedagogies into one's course as a kind of educational intervention because these approaches likely result in a higher probability of students confronting unexpected problems that may result in disorientation. Service learning overlaps with transformative education in significant ways—but this overlap makes me somewhat uneasy. Do I want to purposefully construct learning scenarios that expose students to risks that may be upsetting, even if I believe an emotional response could result in a deeply meaningful, perhaps transformative, learning experience?

In reviewing scholarship on transformative learning, I found very limited coverage of ethics when implementing a purposefully designed transformative education. In the case of McGregor, she critically self-reflects on her own motivations for employing a transformative education that initiates grief before growth: "'What do you get out of this for yourself, by exposing people to a planned loss and hopeful recovery or shift? Are you looking for power, for control?' I am working on that one, with no answer just yet" (McGregor 68). While the transformation McGregor's students experienced was unintentional on her part—she only came to understand their transformation through analysis of freewrites after the class was over—she concludes that she now sees the importance of an educational experience "intentionally designed as a collection of disorienting moments serving to instill a loss leading to shifts in world views" (51). Even still, her reflections suggest an inner turmoil about transformative education.

The writing teachers I interviewed for my study expressed their own concerns about how to balance the risks of community engagement—many of which overlap with components of transformative education—even though they found those pedagogies valuable for student learning. For example, Faith Kurtyka, a graduate teaching assistant at the University of Arizona at the time of our interview, reflected on the risks of students going into the community and her responsibilities to them as the teacher who initiated a service-learning pedagogy: "anything can happen, and I worry about what can happen. ... I feel as a teacher, you're responsible for the things that happen in the classroom, and if bad things happen, that becomes your problem." Kurtyka also noted that she gravitates toward certain kinds of service-learning partnerships because of what she feels comfortable with as a teacher: "I guess I really only did one type of service learning [a partnership with a local school], but that's because of my ethical issues of what do I want students to get involved in or what do I feel like I can manage as a teacher—what do I feel like I can ask them to do that's not too problematic." Kurtyka's comments prompt us to consider how students are implicated by the educational choices we make, such as whether or not to incorporate service learning and in what ways, as well as the responsibilities we have to support them through the learning scenarios we develop.

Another writing teacher I interviewed expressed concerns for students' emotional responses to community-based learning as a result of her own transformative learning experiences. University of Arizona graduate teaching assistant Rachael Wendler said she is committed to critical pedagogies, but she also has reservations about the emotionally-demanding aspects of such approaches: "I really believe in critical pedagogy, and ... I want students to understand structural inequality. But, when I think back to my own experience, ... I came to understand those issues ... in an intensive summer-long [community] program where I had a lot of support. It can be very emotionally demanding to deal with issues of privilege and power, both for students who are new to thinking about these concepts and for those who experience structural inequality in their everyday lives." Wendler's remark highlights the emotions that may arise when we ask students to critically reflect on and engage with issues of privilege, power, and inequity within their communities. While many pedagogues would argue that a degree of discomfort may be productive for student learning, Wendler's reflection reminds us to put ourselves in the shoes of our students and to be mindful of how to provide support through emotional moments in order to lead toward productive learning. In the next section, I analyze an example of a disorienting dilemma from a service-learning course taught by one of the teachers in my study. I use this example to provide a snapshot of the first two phases of Mezirow's theory and to explore the emotional reactions—from the perspective of students, teachers, and community partners—that may accompany disorientation.

Emotional Responses in Community Engagement

In my interview with Rebecca Richards, who at the time was a graduate teaching assistant at the University of Arizona, she told me about her experiences teaching a business writing course that incorporated a service-learning partnership.[4] Richards described how her course design exposed students to increasingly public audiences and experiences. The first assignment was a memo of introduction that students posted to Desire2Learn (a course management system). Students read and responded to each other's memos in ways that Richards described as a kind of "public forum" with "hybrid cyber-interaction" that Richards did not mediate; the public forum created through the online discussion space, though, was closed to a more expansive public beyond the students' peers and teacher. As the semester progressed, students began to engage with more expansive public groups through service-learning partnerships that Richards initiated: "I ... form alliances with non-profit organizations in the community and interview them and establish stakeholder relationships with them across semesters, across years. And then the students ... come in to that relationship and I eventually back out." Students in Richards's business writing course collaborated with the owners of local non-profit organizations to assess organizational writing needs, write a proposal, and work in groups to produce communication "deliverables" that could be used by the organizations.

An additional public component of Richards's course involved students posting reflections about their service-learning experiences to online blogs.[5] She described the blogging assignment as students creating "micro-communities that are more public" (Richards). This assignment required that the students blog about their service-learning project and "invite people in the classroom to join their blog group, read their blog, and comment on it" (Richards). Richards gave students the option of making their blogs public or private, using it as an opportunity to teach audience awareness and differences in writing style and purpose when writing in digital, public contexts. Deciding whether or not to make one's blog public or private—a decision that could change throughout the semester—was something that Richards prompted students to consider carefully. She noted the benefits of "having an online space that can be opened up or closed down" with the possibility of keeping the blog private if the student, for instance, was "having a difficult experience that semester" (Richards). When talking about writing for blogs that students choose to make public, Richards specifically asked students to think about "what kinds of information you should share and what kinds of information you should not share, especially because [students were] blogging about their service-learning project, which [involved] a real person in the community." Having students think about whether and when to go public or stay private with the service-learning blog, noted Richards, was a "good critical thought process for [students] to work out with their collaborators and me."

Despite Richards's recommendation that students carefully consider audience when choosing whether to make their blogs public, she explained that her students were "always surprised when people just show[ed] up on their [public] blog." Richards saw these moments as opportunities to help students reflect on public and professional writing contexts: they were "writing in this different kind of public space," but she used it as a reflective moment inquiring of students: "you've chosen [to make your blog public], and so how does that change your writing?" For one of Richards's students, though, the surprise of a truly more public readership for her blog led to what I argue was a disorienting experience for the student, teacher, and community partner.[6]

When I asked about problems with students going public, Richards described an issue that arose with the public component of the blogging assignment. As the students' experiences, interactions, and writing became increasingly public through service-learning and blogging assignments, the risk of miscommunication, abrupt reactions, and emotional responses also increased. The moment of disorientation for the student, as narrated by Richards, happened during a class session:

> One of my students met with her service-learning client and blogged about the experience—which it was a positive experience—but from it she got the impression that her client ... [seemed] very demanding, hard to please. She wrote in her blog that person's name and put, "My client ... seems like she might be hard to please, so we'll have to work extra hard to make her happy." Well, sure enough, that organization has one of the trackers for looking up on the Web any instance of its organizational name and any of its key stakeholders in that conversation, so [the student's] blog popped up the next day on her client's program. [The client] emailed the student and said, "please do not talk about me in public: if I have given you any reason to think that I am hard to please or difficult, I hope you know I'm committed to this." ... It happened in class that [the student] received the email. ... [The student] blurted out with tears in her eyes "my client's stalking me." (Richards)

I would like to consider this moment of disorientation from a variety of standpoints (e.g., the student's, her peers' in the classroom, the teacher's, and the client's) in the hopes that we may begin to understand the complexity of stakes, responses, and emotions at play here. First, I analyze the student's reaction as a moment of disorientation that has the potential to spark a transformative learning experience.

The student's reaction, as narrated by Richards, represents two key components of the transformative learning process Mezirow theorized: the student experienced a disorienting dilemma with an accompanying emotional response. Receiving the email was clearly disorienting to the student; she may have thought she was being a perceptive observer, using a critical fieldworker's eye to assess her client and the rhetorical context of the service-learning partnership. Indeed, Richards noted that in some ways the student's comment was a fairly "innocuous thing." Richards believed the student "meant no harm by it; she didn't mean this person is impossible to work with, or I don't like this person, or I'm not happy with the project. She just literally was reporting her impressions." For the student who likely thought she was doing a good job of completing her assignment, receiving the emailed reprimand from her client would have been jarring; this would be especially true for a student who Richards described as "a really good student who was conscientious [and] kind."

The student's disorientation was followed by her emotional reaction, what Richards portrayed as the student having "tears in her eyes." Richards interpreted the situation as "painful" for the student; this kind of language maps onto the ways in which Mezirow describes perspective transformation as a potentially painful process (Mezirow, *Transformative Dimensions* 168). Additionally, the student's emotional response aligns with the feelings of "fear, anger, guilt, or shame" that Mezirow theorizes in the second phase of transformative learning. We might conjecture, based on her tearful reaction, that the student may have been feeling angry at the client for sending her an "aggressive email" (Richards); fearful regarding the future of her service-learning partnership, as well as her grade and potential for success in the business writing course; and likely bewildered that the writing on her blog was in fact truly public. The outburst, "my client's stalking me," supports the idea that what was perhaps most disorienting for the student was the public nature of her blog writing, but the word choice of "stalking" also suggests that the student felt betrayed and perhaps threatened. Something about the method through which the client discovered the public writing on the student's blog—the online tracker—may have felt surreptitious to the student, further complicating the situation, mixing in additional layers of emotional response.

If the standpoint is flipped in this scenario, though, we might consider the range of reactions the community partner felt when she discovered the student's public blog. I want to acknowledge that I have very limited data in regards to the community partner in this scenario, but I believe it is productive to consider her possible reactions as well.[7] Based on Richards's explanation of the situation, it seems that the community partner's response demonstrated concern for her public image and the public image of the non-profit organization. It may have been hurtful, even disorienting, for the community partner to read that the student perceived her as being "very demanding, hard to please," especially if she thought that the meeting with the student had gone well and that she was being cordial. Her comments suggest that she was interested in correcting what she saw as the student's misperception of her personality: "if I have given you any reason to think that I am hard to please or difficult, I hope you know that I'm committed to this." Richards described the email as "very aggressive" and noted that, "even though I stepped in at that moment and spoke with the client, told her they're students, they're learning," she was not sure the community partner "ever really got past that," further indicating that the students' words were likely upsetting. Even if the client's email came across as harsh, the overall purpose of it seems to have been to extend an olive branch to the student, to communicate that she wanted to move forward with the partnership, that she was committed to it. Another way to read this community partner's email is as a lesson to the student about the nature of public writing and professional partnerships—exactly what Richards had been trying to get across to her students in the business writing course.

Whether the client purposefully intended it or not, the email came to represent a lesson within Richards's business writing course, in part because of the student's public outburst during class time and because of the way Richards chose to address the situation in the moment. From the perspective of the other students in the class, they were drawn into this student's moment of emotional distress. According to Richards, the student's reaction "created an interesting moment for the class," and she took time to have students work through a response to what had happened: "we unpacked that." Richards's choice to address the student's issue through whole-class discussion transitioned the scenario into a teachable moment, not only for the disoriented student but also for her classmates. Richards could have brushed the student's comment aside, not taking it seriously and thus not validating the student's emotional reaction; she also could have asked the student to see her after class or during office hours to address the issue more privately and/or to give them both more time to process a response. However, Richards's on-the-spot response acknowledged the student's emotional reaction, primed the class for a moment of self-reflection, and, thus, facilitated the scenario as meaningful in terms of learning for the entire class. In our interview, Richards began telling the story as an example of a pitfall, but she ultimately reflected on how the experience was positive for student learning: "I think [the experience] was productive in the end, a good learning lesson for everybody about digital footprints and how [students] go about representing themselves and others in their writing and how that circulates beyond the public that [they] intended it for." Even as Richards expertly handled the moment, validating the students' affective response and helping her and her peers see this as a moment of learning, we might imagine that this was also a challenging moment from her perspective as a teacher.

From Richards's perspective, the student's outburst was somewhat disorienting for her as well. In our interview, Richards reflected that "it took a few minutes for [her] to figure out what had happened; [she questioned], how did this happen?" In recounting the scene, Richards said she was "horrified" for the student, suggesting both her empathy for the student's emotional response but perhaps also her own emotional reaction to the unfolding events. Richards also noted that the student's outburst, combined with the follow-up class discussion, "sort of derailed class for the day," causing her to rearrange her pedagogical plans. Richards's experiences in some ways represent disorienting dilemmas that may be all too familiar to community literacy practitioners. The messiness of engaging with public groups outside of the classroom means that we, as teachers, often have little control over the kind of responses students receive or the kinds of experiences they have in community-based contexts. Indeed, I see this as a productive tension in community-based pedagogies: the possibility for moments of learning that are unexpected, just like the scenario above. What interests me as a teacher who values service learning and community engagement is how we might be able to both anticipate and support affective responses for students, ourselves as teachers, and community partners.

The moment of disorientation I analyzed from Richards's course provides a point from which those of us interested in campus-community partnerships can reflect on how affect and transformation impact teaching and learning in our classrooms. Without further evidence from the student herself, we cannot know whether she was transformed and whether her perspective changed as a result of this experience.[8] We also do not know how the community partner was ultimately impacted by the experience. However, I view this snapshot of the student's experience as important for examining experiences that may spark transformation—experiences that as teachers we might exploit, prompt, avoid, or use as teachable moments. Richards's off-the-cuff decision to use the outburst to facilitate a meaningful learning experience provides an excellent model for community literacy practitioners who may be faced with and/or experiencing disorienting dilemmas. Her response also suggests that in moments of disorientation, teachers have responsibilities to students.

In the final section, I consider how we might employ a reciprocal notion of care in community engagement projects with transformative goals, while avoiding the reinscription of problematic gender-roles. Theories of transformative learning and feminist pedagogy prompt us to break down the divisions constructed by dominant discourses that work to subordinate affect to intellect and women's work to men's work, thwarting efforts to develop a pedagogy of care that would more successfully guide students through processes of transformation. This traditional discourse also replicates gender dualities that read feminist pedagogies of nurturance as women's work (Worsham). One approach for community literacy practitioners who also value feminist pedagogies would be to work to change the discourses of dominant pedagogy by reconstructing conceptions of nurturance and care that are not gender-specific. In what follows, I suggest that some of the concerns raised in regards to transformative learning and education might be addressed by employing tenets of feminist pedagogy, such as decentralizing classroom authority, aiming to empower students as agents in control of their own transformative learning, and transparently challenging them to transform within a context of care.

Decentering Authority, Transparency, and Reciprocal Care

Feminism calls us to be mindful of our positions of power in the classroom and our efforts to subvert those traditionally defined roles. For example, Rebecca Ropers-Huilman, reflecting on teaching her first graduate seminar, explains how she "felt trapped by the constraints of a pedagogy that attempts to enact power in efforts to empower, and care in efforts to ensure comfort, ease, and positive outcomes in learning" (131). The circularity of these feelings reflects many of the dilemmas within transformative education: how can we empower students without exerting power ourselves, and how can we care for students in ways that are not self-serving? Thinking back to McGregor's self-critical line of questioning regarding transformative learning—"What do you get out of this for yourself? ... Are you looking for power, for control?" (68)—we should be prepared to carefully consider our pedagogical choices and what motivations guide those decisions. Moreover, as Ropers-Huilman notes, not all students are interested in the care we may offer. Similarly, Worsham has critiqued the traditional, patriarchal role of the teacher "as the sign of power and the agent of empowerment, as the one who has the power to know students better than they know themselves and to transform their relation to the world" (1020). In transformative education, teachers may be particularly prone to this risk—believing we have the power to transform students' understanding of the world. We, once again, want to empower students, while wanting to avoid exerting power to empower, while also knowing that we can never fully eliminate the power that accompanies our position of authority as the teacher.

I believe we can forge a new path to avoid this circularity by approaching transformative education in community partnerships through (1) reciprocal care that is based on (2) a continual shifting of teacher and learner roles and (3) transparency. Community literacy practitioners familiar with reciprocity know that the give-and-take in community partnerships "need[s] to be openly and consciously negotiated by everyone participating" (Cushman 16). Though not always discussed using the same terminology, reciprocity is a shared value in the feminist classroom. As Ropers-Huilman concludes in her feminist analysis of teaching graduate students: "regardless of the seemingly clear lines between teachers and students in classroom contexts, all educational participants have the ability to enact the power to care" (131). When we consider care in transformative education, especially in community-based projects, I believe reciprocity should be a central value because of its self-critical focus on power relations among students, teachers, and community partners. Without an attention to reciprocity for all participants, we risk abusing our position of authority in the classroom to exert power and control over students or community members—whether that control is through disorientation, transformative education, and/or care. By taking a reciprocal approach, teachers can offer to care for students and community partners, but perhaps more importantly, we can be open to accepting the care that students and community partners may offer to us.

Acknowledging that all participants have the potential for power and the potential to give and receive care can help us move towards decentering authority and shifting teacher and learner roles. Both feminist classrooms and community engagement projects attempt to shift the loci of power and authority, positioning students and community partners as teachers and teachers as learners, blurring traditionally-defined roles. The opening up and shifting of teacher and learner positions is unlikely to happen in a classroom where the teacher does not present herself as ready to learn and, at times, vulnerable. As hooks emphasizes in *Teaching to Transgress*, "engaged pedagogy does not seek simply to empower students. Any classroom that employs a holistic model of learning will also be a place where teachers grow, and are empowered by the process" (21). Integral to this holistic model of empowerment is that teachers are open to being "vulnerable while encouraging students to take risks" (hooks 21). Presenting oneself as a learner who may be just as vulnerable as a student and community partner may seem too risky to some pedagogues; but, if we support a model of reciprocal care, we can hope that our students and community partners will offer the support we need in moments of disorientation or distress.

In order to be attentive to the dynamics of power and reciprocity, I believe we must also strive to be transparent with students and community partners. In her self-reflections, McGregor questions the extent to which teachers should prepare students for the grief that may accompany transformation; she questions whether telling students they will go through fairly predictable stages of "grief toward growth" would have a negative impact on their transformation. Feminist pedagogies value transparency in the classroom, and I believe that the most ethical approach to transformative education is to be open and honest with students, sharing our misgivings and enthusiasm for the processes we may experience with them. A transparent approach to teaching service learning might involve telling students from the start that we do not know exactly what will transpire over the course of the semester or how they might respond. In fact, I have started including the following disclaimer on my service-learning syllabi to that effect:

> Having taught service-learning courses in the past, I can assure you that there will be many unknowns. I will not be able to tell you exactly how your experiences and assignments will unfold because they will develop through your interactions with our community partners. The unknowns of the process can be disconcerting for some students, but, as long as you keep an open line of communication with me and your community partner, we will be able to work through things so that you can succeed in the course assignments. (Holmes, "English 3120")

This disclaimer on my syllabus functions as a kind of trigger warning for students, even though I am not able to identify what the triggers may be. In fact, in their critique of mandated trigger warnings, seven humanities professors identify the number one flaw with a proposed mandate as the fact that "faculty cannot predict in advance what will be triggering for students" (Freeman et al.). While I agree with many concerns faculty have raised in regards to censoring course content, requiring trigger warnings on syllabi, and protecting untenured and non-tenure track faculty, I also believe that we have responsibilities to be transparent and care for students when we employ pedagogies that may be risky and disorienting. However, we also must be willing to "share our struggles with students as we negotiate relationships supported and disrupted by power and caring practices" (Ropers-Huilman 133). When we share our struggles, students have a better sense of how we as teacher-learners experience disorienting dilemmas and move toward transformation.

Though I am still honing what it means to enact a reciprocal model of care in courses where I incorporate service- or community-based learning, I can offer a brief example from a recent graduate course I taught at Georgia State University called Public Rhetorics for Social Change. One component of the course involved a collaborative "public project" that I did not define for students, in part as an attempt to decenter my authority and in part to provide a context for students to experience the messy and challenging process of finding a meaningful public with which to engage. I tried to be transparent with students at the start of the semester, noting on the syllabus that I did not know what this project would ultimately look like but that we would work together to define how they would contribute and be assessed. After months of discussions about possible prison literacy initiatives or direct service to non-profit organizations, the class decided they/we wanted to lead a series of group discussions (modeled on Linda Flower's intercultural communication strategies) about the experiences of international students with writing on campus. I sent a collaboratively-drafted query on behalf of the class to a faculty member in another department who we considered a stakeholder and who we hoped might be an ally for us in this public project, but our good intentions were either unwanted or ill-received as the faculty member responded by telling our group about all the programs already in place to help non-native speakers transition into college writing. The email response was upsetting and disorienting to me, in part because the faculty member rhetorically positioned herself as expert and our class (and by extension me) as novices—noting the dozens of world-renowned books and articles she and her colleagues had published on non-native speakers and college writing—but also because I felt our intentions had been misunderstood. We were hoping to collaborate and partner, but the response we received suggested we were stepping on toes, questioning the effectiveness of programs already in place, and/or overstepping our bounds.

During the next class, I tried to be transparent in explaining why I would suggest we move in a different direction for the project. This level of transparency, as I reflect back, made me vulnerable to my students: I noted my concerns about "rocking the boat" by moving forward with the project because I was a newcomer to the campus community, a pre-tenure faculty member, and not an expert in scholarship on composition theories related to Teaching English as a Second Language. I also conveyed my disappointment and frustration that I felt hemmed in by these institutional constructs, and I emphasized that my vote was only one vote, that I would help the class move forward with whatever project we came to agree upon. Ultimately, the class moved in a different direction, choosing a supportive in-house partner within the Lower Division Studies program.[9] I believe that the process our class went through of reacting to the disorienting email aligns with a reciprocal model of care. I attempted to care for students by shepherding a project that they would be invested in and promoting reflection on why we received such a negative reaction to our originally proposed project. The graduate students in the course offered their care for me both in terms of how they carefully considered the complex demands on me as their instructor and how they negotiated with each other and me to decide on a project that would meet our needs in the course and fulfill their interests in public rhetorics.

In many ways, this is a story of my own transformation as a teacher who employs community-based and service learning pedagogies. As I think back to the interviews I conducted with writing teachers, I realize how their narratives prompted me to transform my pedagogical approach by being mindful of the affective components of community-based projects and by shifting to a more transparent and de-centered role in the classroom. And, as I begin another semester of service-learning partnerships, I have already begun considering how I might prompt students to critically self-reflect in ways that may lead to transformative learning. However, I also approach these transformative goals with a mindfulness of the unknowns of the real world contact zone and the emotional responses that may emerge for students. A reciprocal and feminist approach to transformative, community-based education reminds us that we are all learners who need to be challenged and supported. When we position ourselves as learners, teachers, and care-takers, inviting students and community partners to do the same, the traditional gender-basis of those roles becomes further removed, and we begin to see the potential for a truly transformative experience.

Endnotes

1. I use "real world" in quotes here to acknowledge that while the classroom space is certainly part of the real world, I tend to agree with scholars who have demonstrated how university classroom spaces can be removed from surrounding communities in ways that make the everyday issues that emerge in those spaces feel contrived (Cushman and Emmons; Grabill; Heilker). I do not want to set up a false dichotomy between classroom and real world. However, my advocacy of community engagement projects lies in what I see as their power to access and value public, non-school sites for student learning.

2. For this study, I conducted interviews with 19 writing teachers and administrators, including tenure track and non-tenure track faculty, graduate teaching assistants, and writing program administrators. The study received IRB approval at each of the three institutions, and each interviewee gave me informed consent to use her name (though participants were given an option to use a pseudonym) and to quote from our interview. Additionally, participants were given the opportunity to read drafts of my writing to ensure the ways in which I represented them and their pedagogy were accurate.

3. The complete list of the ten phases of Mezirow's original theory of transformative learning are as follows: (1) a disorienting dilemma, (2) self-examination with feelings of fear, anger, guilt, or shame, (3) a critical assessment of assumptions, (4) recognition that one's discontent and the process of transformation are shared, (5) exploration of options for new roles, relationships, and actions, (6) planning a course of action, (7) acquiring knowledge and skills for implementing one's plans, (8) provisional trying of new roles, (9) building competence and self-confidence in new roles and relationships, and (10) a reintegration into one's life on the basis of conditions dictated by one's new perspective (Mezirow, *Learning as Transformation*).

4. Because I offer an in-depth analysis of an example from Richards's interview, I want readers to know that Richards read several drafts of this manuscript, offering feedback and confirmation on how I represent her and analyze her pedagogy.

5. As community literacy practitioners well know, reflection has been theorized as an important component of learning for professionals (Schön), for students in the writing classroom (Yancey), and for students engaging in service learning (Ash, Atkinson, and Clayton). Critical self-reflection is also a significant component of transformative learning theory (Mezirow).

6. In a recently published article on cyberfeminist pedagogy in *Feminist Teacher*, Richards discusses a different dilemma that arose in her business-writing course with a service-learning component (see Richards, "I Could Have Told You").

7. I want to underscore that the lack of community partner perspectives is a significant issue within community literacy and service-learning scholarship—an issue that has been noted and has begun to be addressed by Marie Sandy and Barbara A. Holland's research on community partner perspectives, as well as Randy Stoecker and Elizabeth A. Tryon's edited collection *The Unheard Voices: Community Organizations and Service Learning*.

8. Moreover, collecting the kind of evidence that would document and track a student's transformation is particularly challenging because the process could take years; the stu-

dent may experience an emotional trigger that she continues to reflect on and unpack for months or years to come (Mezirow). Despite these challenges, this is an area ripe for future research—tracking whether and how students transform after service-learning experiences.

9. I think it is important to acknowledge that the "public" with which the class ended up partnering (an on-campus group) did not fall within what many teacher-scholars would define as a traditional community partnership, which often involves partnering with an off-campus group that may or may not be a non-profit organization. Within the graduate seminar, students read and engaged with theories of public(s) and counterpublic(s), and much of our discussion centered on defining and locating public(s). After careful consideration of the constraints of our one-semester commitment to a project, the class decided to draw on our already-existing knowledge of the campus community and the first-year writing curriculum in order to contribute a one-time project, rather than initiate an unsustainable project with a community partner off-campus. The resulting "public project" was a collaboratively-written chapter, titled "Civic Engagement and Community-Based Writing," for the custom published first-year writing textbook and a corresponding online resource guide for writing instructors interested in incorporating civic engagement, service learning, and/or community-based writing into their courses.

Works Cited

Ash, Sarah L., Maxine P. Atkinson, and Patti H. Clayton. "Integrating Reflection and Assessment to Capture and Improve Student Learning." *Michigan Journal of Community Service Learning* 11.2 (2005): 49–60. *Academic OneFile*. Web. 4 Sept. 2011.

Cooper, Jan. Personal Interview via Skype. 27 Apr. 2011.

Cushman, Ellen. "The Rhetorician as an Agent of Social Change." *College Composition and Communication* 47.1 (1996): 7–28. *JSTOR*. Web. 22 Jan. 2010.

Cushman, Ellen, and Chalon Emmons. "Contact Zones Made Real." *School's Out: Bridging Out-of-School Literacies with Classroom Practice*. Ed. Glyda Hull and Katherine Schultz. New York: Teachers College Press, 2002. 203–232. Print.

Cushman, Ellen, and Erik Green. "Knowledge Work with the Cherokee Nation." *The Public Work of Rhetoric: Citizen-Scholars and Civic Engagement*. Ed. John M. Ackerman and David J. Coogan. Columbia, SC: U of South Carolina P, 2010. 175–192. Print.

DeGenaro, William. "The Affective Dimensions of Service Learning." *Reflections: Writing, Service-Learning, and Community Literacy* 9.3 (Summer 2010): 192–220. Print.

Felten, Peter, and H-Dirksen L. Bauman. "Reframing Diversity and Student Engagement: Lessons from Deaf-Gain." *The Student Engagement Handbook: Practices in Higher Education*. Ed. Elisabeth Dunne and Derfel Owen. Bingley, UK: Emerald Group Publishing, 2013. 367–379. Print.

Festinger, Leon. *A Theory of Cognitive Dissonance*. Stanford: Stanford UP, 1957. Print.

Flower, Linda. *Community Literacy and the Rhetoric of Public Engagement.* Carbondale: Southern Illinois UP, 2008. Print.

Fodrey, Crystal. Personal Interview. 28 Apr. 2011.

Freeman, Elizabeth, Brian Herrera, Nat Hurley, Homay King, Dana Luciano, Dana Seitler, and Patricia White. "Trigger Warnings Are Flawed." *Inside Higher Ed.* 29 May 2014. Web. 20 June 2014.

Grabill, Jeffrey T. *Writing Community Change: Designing Technologies for Citizen Action.* New Dimensions in Computers and Composition. Cresskill, NJ: Hampton Press, 2007. Print.

Guile, David, and Michael Young. "Transfer and Transition in Vocational Education." *Between School and Work: New Perspectives on Transfer and Boundary-crossing.* Ed. Terttu Tuomi-Gröhn and Yrjö Engeström. Amsterdam: Pergamon, 2003. 63–84. Print.

Heilker, Paul. "Rhetoric Made Real: Civic Discourse and Writing Beyond the Curriculum." *Writing the Community: Concepts and Models for Service-Learning in Composition.* Ed. Linda Adler-Kassner, Robert Crooks, and Ann Watters. Washington, DC: AAHE and NCTE, 1997. 71–78. Print.

Holmes, Ashley J. "Public Pedagogy and Writing Program Administration: A Comparative, Cross-Institutional Study of Going Public in Rhetoric and Composition." Diss. University of Arizona, 2012.

——. English 3120: Digital Writing & Publishing. Syllabus. 2013. Web. 23 May 2014. <http://3120fall2013.wordpress.com/about/service-learning/>.

hooks, bell. *Teaching to Transgress: Education as the Practice of Freedom.* New York: Routledge, 2000. Print.

Karpiak, Irene E. "Evolutionary Theory and the 'New Sciences': Rekindling Our Imagination for Transformation." *Studies in Continuing Education* 22.1 (2000): 29–44. EBSCOhost Academic Search Complete. Web. 9 June 2013.

Kurtyka, Faith. Personal Interview. 27 Apr. 2011.

McGregor, Sue L. T. "Transformative Education: Grief and Growth." *Narrating Transformative Learning in Education.* Ed. Morgan Gardner and Ursula Kelly. New York: Palgrave Macmillan, 2008. 51–74. Print.

Medina, Jennifer. "Warning: The Literary Canon Could Make Students Squirm." *The New York Times.* 17 May 2014. Web. 1 June 2014.

Mezirow, Jack. *Transformative Dimensions of Adult Learning.* San Francisco: Jossey-Bass, 1991. Print.

Mezirow, Jack, and Associates. *Learning as Transformation: Critical Perspectives on a Theory in Progress.* San Francisco: Jossey-Bass, 2000. Print.

Piaget, Jean. *Six Psychological Studies.* Trans. Anita Tenzer. Ed. David Elkind. New York: Random House, 1967. Print.

Richards, Rebecca. "'I Could Have Told You That Wouldn't Work': A Cyberfeminist Pedagogy in Action." *Feminist Teacher* 22.1 (2011): 5–22. JSTOR. Web. 14 June 2013.

——. Personal Interview. 20 Apr. 2011.

Ropers-Huilman, Rebecca. "Scholarship on the Other Side: Power and Caring in Feminist Education." *NWSA Journal* 11.1 (1999): 118–35. *JSTOR*. Web. 14 Feb. 2013.
Sandy, Marie, and Barbara A. Holland. "Different Worlds and Common Ground: Community Partner Perspectives on Campus-Community Partnerships." *Michigan Journal of Community Service Learning* 13.1 (Fall 2006): 30–43. Print.
Schneider, Barbara. "Uncommon Ground: Narcissistic Reading and Material Racism." Pedagogy 5.2 (2005): 195-212. Rpt. in *The Norton Book of Composition Studies*. Ed. Susan Miller. New York: Norton, 2009. 919–932. Print.
Schön, Donald. *The Reflective Practitioner: How Professionals Think in Action*. United States: Basic Books, 1984. Print.
Scott, Sue M. "The Grieving Soul in the Transformation Process." *New Directions for Adult and Continuing Education* 74 (1997): 41–50. *EBSCOhost Academic Search Complete*. Web. 10 June 2013.
Stoecker, Randy, and Elizabeth A. Tryon, eds. *The Unheard Voices: Community Organizations and Service Learning*. Philadelphia, PA: Temple UP, 2009. Print.
Tuomi-Gröhn, Terttu, and Yrjö Engeström. "Conceptualizing Transfer: From Standard Notions to Developmental Perspectives." *Between School and Work: New Perspectives on Transfer and Boundary-crossing*. Ed. Terttu Tuomi-Gröhn and Yrjö Engeström. Amsterdam: Pergamon, 2003. 19–38. Print.
Wendler, Rachael. Personal Interview. 27 Apr. 2011.
Worsham, Lynn. "Going Postal: Pedagogic Violence and the Schooling of Emotion." *Journal of Advanced Composition* 18.2 (1998): 213–245. Rpt. in *The Norton Book of Composition Studies*. Ed. Susan Miller. New York: Norton, 2009. 999–1031. Print.
Yancey, Kathleen Blake. *Reflection in the Writing Classroom*. Logan: Utah State UP, 1998. Print.

Author Bio:

Ashley J. Holmes's research explores how the lens of publics can help composition and rhetoric scholars productively theorize, historicize, and relocate writing pedagogy within community-based contexts beyond the classroom or campus. She is currently working on a book-length manuscript that argues for public approaches to pedagogy and administration based on comparative analysis of three case studies conducted within the writing programs at Oberlin College, Syracuse University, and the University of Arizona. Holmes has published articles in *Reflections, English Journal*, and *Kairos*, and she is currently an assistant editor with the refereed, open-access online journal *Kairos: A Journal of Rhetoric Technology, and Pedagogy*.

Translingual Communities: Teaching and Learning Where You Don't Know the Language

Elizabeth Kimball

In fields such as sociolinguistics and composition and rhetoric, communication is increasingly understood as translingual, that is, as negotiated socially across languages. Those of us engaged in community literacy can and should recognize the deeply multilingual nature of the communities in which we work, and we should understand, embrace, and forward the translingual approach. Here I reflect on my first conscious attempt to teach translingually in a college course with a community-based learning component. I present an overview of the translingual orientation, reflect on the decisions I made as I prepared a college community-based learning course with translingual intentions but not overt translingual objectives, and examine some the students' reflections that reveal their language attitudes at the end of the course. I argue that small, intentional decisions made towards a broader translingual orientation towards language and literacy make an immediate difference in how students think about language, and that those engaged in community literacy partnerships are in need of a theory of communication that the translingual approach can provide.

Keywords: community-based learning; translingual; language learning; Latino communities; college teaching; reflective practice; adult literacy

Introduction

Those of us who are engaged in community literacy, by virtue of the work we do, foster a belief in the possibility of communicating across a wide range of semiotic spheres. The artist in community does not only wish to create art for other artists, or art theorists, but for and with the community; the community theater collaborative generates dramatic works out of the concerns and voices of the community, not a select, well-heeled theater-going subculture. University-trained intellectuals working in collaboration with local citizens and organizations do not, at the end of the day, see talking only to other university-trained intellectuals as worthwhile. We believe that knowledge may be generated and shared across communities, rather than only within them.

We share this outlook as readers of *Community Literacy Journal*. Although we may not always refer to it directly, I suspect many of us talk about this boundary crossing in a shorthand kind of way, often using the expression of "speaking other languages." We don't really mean other languages, we think, but we know what we mean when we feel able to communicate easily with a particular person, group, or community. We might also be thinking of the different kinds of talk we move in and out of in the course of a day: in a religious service, we might feel comfortable speaking a language of God and the spirit; in a budget meeting, we would feel comfortable speaking a language of dollars and cents. Some of us might be good at code switching, taking on different dialects or styles of English, or even hybrid varieties like Spanglish, when we move from one community to another. We probably mean something closer to the specialized term "discourse communities" when we use the phrase "speaking a language" in this way, but nevertheless, it is the term "language" that we naturally turn to in an everyday sense. In other words, we often talk about languages figuratively, rather than literally.

But the figurative idea of language raises questions about the boundary between the figurative and the literal. What if this figurative understanding of the ability to speak other languages were also literally true? A truly egalitarian, pluralist democracy would require us to listen to one another well outside the borderlines of English, wouldn't it? Could a fully realized community literacy be truly multilingual? Many linguists and literacy specialists, in recognition of the practices of people around the world, are beginning to argue that borders between languages are only imagined. This "translingual" understanding challenges the notion that languages constitute discrete systems, distinct from one another in grammar and vocabulary and, perhaps more significantly, in their alignment with cultures and nations.[1] Today, in linguistics and related fields such as composition and rhetoric, communication is increasingly understood as translingual, that is, as negotiated socially within and across languages in such a way as to discard the very notion of discrete, monolithic, grammar-based systems such as English or Spanish.

How might an understanding of a translingual approach aid us in the work of community literacy? I argue that attending to the translingual facets of communication as we engage university and community partners can bring about changes in attitude and ultimately in what we are able to accomplish together. But we need not make a complicated-sounding term like "the translingual approach" into a direct topic of discussion. Instead, we can pursue it indirectly, using familiar terms that people already understand. In the discussion that follows, I further explore what the concept means and how even monolingual people can participate in it. Then I reflect on how I did so in the context of a course I taught at my small liberal arts college, in which English monolingual college students came together in learning with Spanish-speaking community members. While I hope that this discussion is of practical use to others pursuing similar teaching situations, it should understood more broadly as an argument for the reality of dialogue across languages of all sorts, and an introduction to a theory of communication that can improve community literacy practice.

Translingualism in Practice and in Attitude

Simply put, a translingual approach allows us "to consider all acts of communication and literacy as involving a shuttling between languages and a negotiation of diverse linguistic resources for situated construction of meaning" and "to treat communication as an alignment of words with many other semiotic resources involving different symbol systems (i.e., icons, images), modalities of communication (i.e., aural, oral, visual, and tactile channels), and ecologies (i.e., social and material contexts of communication)" (Canagarajah 2013, 1).[2] Translingualism is a practiced phenomena, and it can be observed in all kinds of settings, particularly sites around the world where languages come in contact, such as national borders, postcolonial nations, and cultures that harbor a diversity of indigenous local languages: in any kind of contact zone. It is not exclusively associated with multilingual regions, but it is a theory that grows out of those kinds of places: Gloria Anzaldúa's writing, for example, can be considered translingual, because it draws on English and Spanish, and hybrid varieties, for rhetorical power. Translingual practice is also observable in online venues in which people must negotiate with a broader range of linguistic possibility than in their local material worlds, and thus is practiced by those who would otherwise consider themselves monolingual, such as monolingual suburban American teenagers (Canagarajah 2013, 5, citing Wiliams 2009). To communicate translingually is to adopt a variety of creative strategies to communicate in the absence of shared linguistic structures. For instance, translingualists enjoy what Firth calls the "let it pass principle," simply ignoring grammatical oddities and lapses in understanding in favor of getting the sense and intention of the message over time. In other words, anybody has the capacity for translingual communication, regardless of his or her language background or so-called bilingual or multilingual proficiency–themselves terms that are debunked by the translingual approach, as they invoke a monolingual proficiency in more than one language.

But besides an observable practice, a translingual approach is also an orientation to language that may be studied, reflected on, and adopted by those of us who speak and write from monolingualist legacies.[3] In that sense, a translingual approach does for language what theories of white privilege do for race: it helps those of us who enjoy privilege recognize that we possess it; and it makes race, or in this case language, a thing that is owned by everyone rather than an add-on category to a core version of humanity, an unmarked version that only the privileged can be. While we cannot stop being the race that we are, given race's reification in culture, we can reconsider what it means to have been "born" one race or another, and, over the years, to adjust the way we interact with the world accordingly.[4] Likewise, we can begin adopting a translingual attitude even before we acquire increased creativity and flexibility in using linguistic codes, before we become more multilingual and less monolingual. For instance, we can begin working with the questions put forth by Horner, Lu, Royster, and Trimbur: "When faced with difference in language, this approach asks: What might this difference do? How might it function expressively, rhetorically, and communicatively? For whom, under what conditions, and how?" (303-304). We can drop the question that we are accustomed to asking: does this person speak English like I do?

A translingual approach, then, contributes a usable theory of communication to pedagogical movements in experiential learning and community and critical literacy. These movements represent attempts to create partnerships that are more just and egalitarian. A translingual approach helps us because community literacy compels us to engage, and it offers us a means to do so, in places where so-called Standard English, or indeed any kind of English, is not spoken. If language and literacy in all its forms, both linguistic and more broadly semiotic, are understood not as residing in individuals but in the act of creative negotiation of meaning, then we have a tool with which to discard inherited hierarchies of the literate and non-literate, and the (native) English-speaking and non (native)-English speaking, as well as, for example, the artist and non–artist, or the academic and non–academic. This understanding is particularly important in many university-community partnerships in diverse communities, where we want to connect despite language difference. I have been thinking about this issue a great deal as I teach in an English department and work to get my students thinking about language and meaning in the community: a community that is, in fact, Spanish-speaking. Should I leave that partnership work to the Spanish department? I don't think so. I want my students to act translingually, even if they don't know Spanish.

Consider how the translingual approach enriches the work that has been done in university-community literacy partnerships. Adopting the guidelines for "promoting productive learning for all involved," Eli Goldblatt's adaptation of Saul Alinsky's organizing model for university-community partnerships, a translingual approach could, for example "respect people's dignity by creating the conditions for them to be active participants in solving their own problems rather than victims or mere recipients of aid" (320). A translingual attitude would mean that being an "active participant" means communicating as a speaker who has full command of language rather than limited command of the "target" language. Similarly, to "draw on the inevitability of class and group conflict as well as the unpredictability of events for your creativity to invent tactics that fit the moment" (320) would be to draw on the widest possible range of communicative resources, setting aside concerns for cognitive access to the textbook grammar construction or the best word. It would be to invent *language* that fits the moment. And as I argue here, "try to see every situation in as stark a light as possible, unblurred by ideological imperatives, traditional hatreds, or conventional moralities" (320). Horner, Trimbur, Lu, Royster and the others who have termed the translingual approach have done so in such a way to help us avoid falling into another –ism. They write, "while increasing one's linguistic resources is always beneficial, taking a translingual approach is not about the number of languages, or language varieties, one can claim to know. Rather, it is about the disposition of openness and inquiry that people take toward language and language differences" (311). I am not merely advocating multilingual*ism* but rather a particular "disposition" that allows us to encounter the profound reality of language difference as meaningfully as we in community literacy have tried to encounter the profound realities of difference in race, class, education, gender, and the like.

Teaching with a Translingual Attitude

The trouble with working in communities of language difference is that people do, for good and practical reasons, understand languages as distinct. The language barrier is, for most Americans, a real and objective thing. My students would be no different. I knew that I needed to recruit students for the course using language they could understand, and then I would wait and see how much of a translingual approach I could introduce in time. The students would be serving as volunteer tutors and conversation partners in an evening ESOL course at a local community center, and many of the community students would know little English. The community students would come from the local Latino/a population, immigrants of a range of literacy and class backgrounds from Guatemala, Honduras, Colombia, and Peru. We wanted to shift the relationship from tutor-student to partners on as level ground as possible, which we would enable by involving everyone in a bilingual oral history project. The college students would collect oral histories from the community students, transcribe them, and then edit and revise them collectively with the community students. We would collect the documents into a printed book for all to have as a keepsake of the experience. Without extensive preparation in TESOL (Teaching English as a Second or Other Language), or with any Spanish of their own, or with a class carefully prepared by a professional ESL teacher, could my English monolingual students contribute all that much?

I believed that they could. But I knew that I could not force the idea on them. With all the other moving parts to manage in a community-based learning course, I would not think of suggesting to my students that their English monolingualism, and the community members' Spanish monolingualism, would not be a challenge. Nor would I think of specializing the course content to such a degree that the study of translingual practice, still being investigated at the research level, would be the main content of a sophomore-level general education course, with a host of learning outcomes to achieve (it was both a designated community-based learning course as well as writing intensive).

But I did want to introduce students to theories about literacy and language, and to debunk myths about immigrants and literacy, the ease of English language learning, and English-only ideologies. We would also be running our course in the same time slot as a course in Spanish taught by my friend and colleague Elise DuBord, and her students would be participating in the same evening ESOL classes. Thus, we would have people coming together one evening a week from three different literacy and language cultures: English-speaking college students, Spanish-speaking and English-speaking college students, and Spanish-speaking community members–although such labels do little to explain the diversity of language and literacy backgrounds, nor of their current status as language learners. No two kinds of language proficiency, language variety, literacy, or experience would be shared. I wanted my own students to start thinking translingually, and then acting translingually as best as they could, even though I knew they would not become speakers of Spanish in a few short hours in an off-campus experience. The three leaders of the project –the education coordinator at the local community center, my colleague in the Spanish department, and I got together and planned an oral history project that would enable all the members of the community to work together towards a common goal: a bilingual book that everyone would be able to take home as a document and keepsake of the experience. That way, we would begin to erase the notions of language experts and novices, and the hierarchies that that entails.

I called the course "Community Language and Literacy" and framed out its motivating questions in as friendly language as I could. Here's the text from a flyer I posted around campus:

ENGL 219 001 **Community Language and Literacy**

Prof. Elizabeth Kimball MW 10:40AM-11:55AM
Students must also be available Tues or Thurs 7-9PM

Community Language and Literacy explores how people learn about language and learn to read. You'll learn about

- The range of programs and curricula for teaching literacy in the community
- How to tutor and work with language learners
- How linguistic ideologies affect our practices in teaching literacy

Alongside classroom work, you will serve as a tutor in an evening course in English as a Second Language offered at Morristown Neighborhood House, and participate in a community-wide project to record literacy and immigration stories of participants.

This class is a special course that may not be offered again!

Build your resume...connect with people in a bilingual environment...be an active learner!

Students must choose one "lab" section per week, Tuesday or Thursday evenings from 7-9 pm, and allow time in their schedules to get to Morristown. Gen Ed: WRIT (writing intensive), OFFC

Questions? Contact me...Liz Kimball...lkimball@drew.edu

---

figure 1. flyer for Community Language and Literacy course

I wanted to explain the content and the activities in words that my students would not only understand, but get excited about. It was not for me to critique the monolingualist assumptions in the English-language classes for adults, nor could I pretend that a student would not take this class merely for a better chance at getting a job once out of college, or to get the off-campus credit he or she needed to graduate. Instead, I tried to build on these familiar motivations and work into them some translingualist approaches:

• I used the word "bilingual," even though it is ideologically distinct from a translingual approach, and emphasized that the off-campus component would be an exciting challenge to work with people who don't share the same language proficiency in English. I talked about how we would learn from our own struggles to communicate just as the English-language learners would, and that we all had the capacity to connect with others. In my vocabulary, then, I approached translingualism indirectly, "slant," as Emily Dickinson might have said. I just wanted students to find the courage to go where English is not dominant, and then to find out what comes next.

• I talked up the oral history project we had planned, which also drew a number of students who saw themselves as writers, or who expressed interest in narrative. This exercise, in which my English students, my colleague's college Spanish students, and the community center's adult students worked together to record and translate the community students' life stories, was the most translingual experience of the semester, in that language as a mode of communication (rather than a subject of study) was brought into the foreground as the participants crafted interview questions, listened, talked, transcribed, translated, and edited the stories. Participants were acting translingually, even if they did not know it.

• I emphasized how students were building professional skills. We brought in a TESOL specialist to give students strategies for working as language tutors, emphasizing that TESOL is a professional field with career opportunities they might consider. We also held regular reflective discussions to talk about how events were playing out at the center: how should student volunteers understand their relationship to adult community volunteers? What kind of agency could a college volunteer seize in planning lessons or taking charge in a tutoring session? How did you find ways to communicate something without having the exact words you wanted? These discussions, I hope, fostered an awareness of ways of being in civic, professional, and cross-cultural settings, and since the translingual approach recognizes that language is embedded in social and bodily ways of being, I think I can claim that at least, the spirit of the translingual approach was honored.

But could students really buy into the core of the translingual approach, this radical idea that language barriers are only imaginary? That core concept, I realized as the semester went on, makes everything else possible: it frees us to do that collaborative work, which in this case took the form of language learning and the producing of written texts. Eventually I broached the subject in several class periods of reading discussion in the latter half of the semester. I continued to take an indirect approach: rather than assigning readings about translingualism that were likely too specialized for undergraduate general education students, I assigned a selection of personal language memoirs, all of them favorites of many an undergraduate anthology: Amy Tan's "Mother Tongue," Malcolm X's "Learning to Read" from his *Autobiography*, Sandra Cisneros' "Only Daughter," an excerpt from Richard Rodriguez's *Hunger of Memory*, and for its political significance and rhetorical complexity, Gloria Anzaldúa's "How to Tame a Wild Tongue." After a month or two of readings in sociolinguistics and the history of literacy, these first-person narratives were welcome by all of us.

Eventually we reached a level of understanding that let me ask a question of application and signficance: if we often talk about a language barrier, and we envision that barrier as a tall, solid wall between one language and another, how do each of these authors seem to resist, work around, or reinvent that metaphor? I drew a wall on the board and let students think about representations of the language barrier. Soon, they began generating ideas: you can fly over a wall, like a bird; you can dig under it, like a prisoner; you can blast a hole in it, like a radical activist. I pushed them to link these images to the metaphors that seem implied by each author. Here is a picture of what resulted:

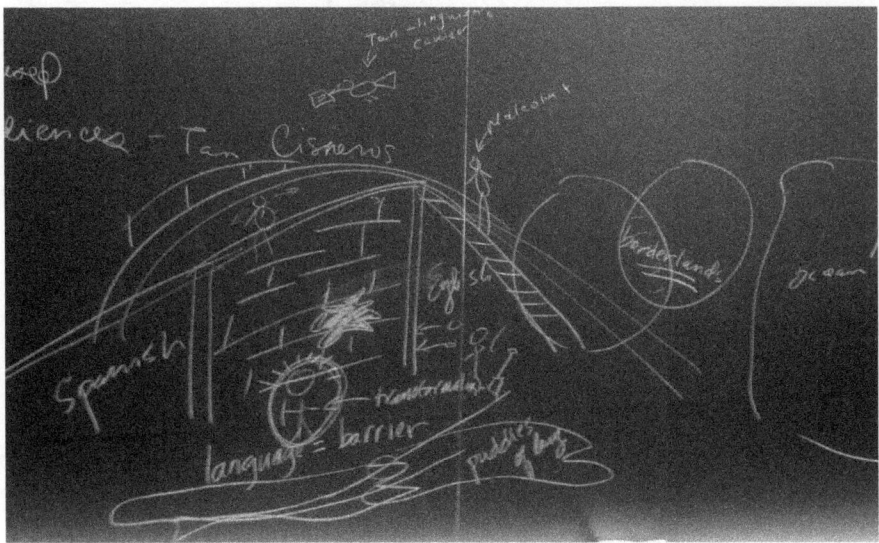

figure 2.

I was delighted. Still, my students accepted the wall image without comment. Their metaphors overcame the barrier, but the barrier still existed, suggesting that overcoming was something to be done only by individuals, and creative, hard-working ones at that, like the talented people who wrote these narratives. What about their own ordinary U.S. monolingual selves? For them, other languages would remain on the other side of a high, thick wall. They would not learn Spanish well enough, at least not in this setting, to really talk in-depth with the community participants.

Keeping what I had learned about a translingual approach in mind, I proposed an alternative: what if we thought about languages as oceans? We can draw a line on the ground to separate the U.S. from Mexico, and with English from Spanish. But where does the North Atlantic end and the South Atlantic begin? At what point is the Atlantic Ocean the New York harbor or the Chesapeake Bay? Is the water in one part markedly different from the water in the other part?

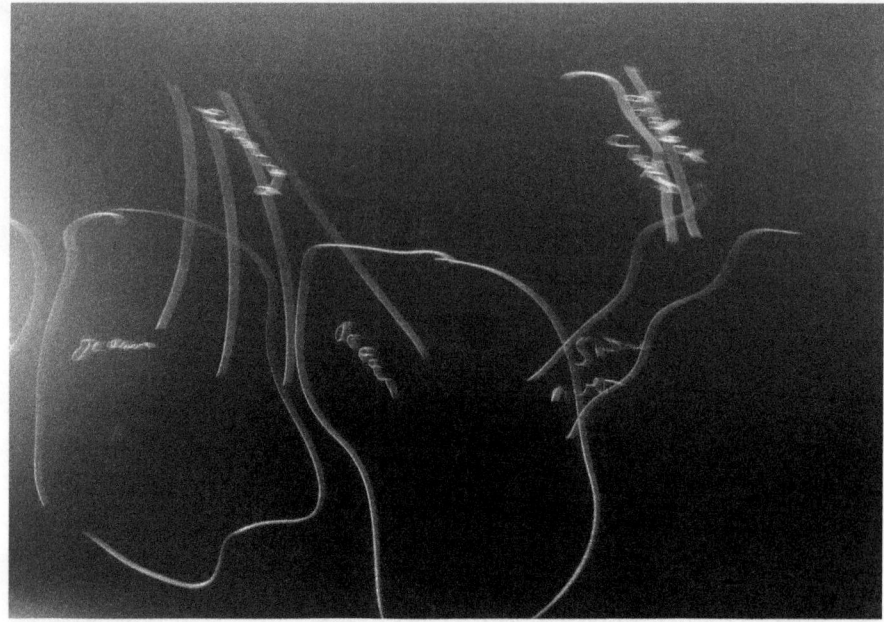

figure 3.

Thinking about this kind of metaphor for language was hard for my students, and I can understand why because I too am a monolingual U.S. citizen, albeit one who has tried to overcome that inheritance. If languages were the same, it would not be so hard to learn a new one, and it would not be so hard to communicate with others who do not speak the same language, or at least not to degree that the speaker does. The absence of detail in my visual metaphor of the ocean reflects the relative absence of verbal response to my idea.

Translingual Thinking in Student Reflections

While I was not interested in indoctrinating students in a translingual attitude, then, nor did I introduce the concept until the very end of the course, I did hope that all our careful planning of collaborative literacy in the community would lead to students' being more thoughtful about what language and literacy are and how they mediate both everyday interactions and broader cultural hierarchies. In collaboration with my colleague in Spanish, we designed a series of prompts for reflection essays that would be assigned to both of our classes at the beginning, middle, and end of the course. While I cannot proffer a complete assessment within the confines of this article, I discerned a pattern of responses upon reading the complete set of reflection essays that were written at the conclusion of the course.

I divide the responses into two categories. The first is students' sensitivity toward language learning. I wanted to know how students thought about language itself and language learning: did the course and the community experience help them to develop complex views of language, and of the people who try to acquire language as adults? While my course focused explicitly on this topic—one of our course texts was Ana Celia Zentella's *Building on Strength: Language and Literacy in Latino Families and Communities*—my colleague's did not; her course examined the immigrant experience. What we found, then, is that while my students found more language for describing language, because that's what we'd been reading and writing about semester, both groups of students developed sensitivity to, and respect for, the enormous undertaking of becoming bilingual in adulthood. Students displayed awareness of language as a symbolic system rather than a transparent reflection of reality; they recognized that it encompassed more than grammatical fixity; and they revealed their own willingness to "go with the flow":

Here are some of the words of students:

> Within the ESOL classes at Neighborhood House, I have learned that people need support while language learning, that most language learners have complicated histories, and for me to use the language barrier to my advantage while volunteering at the neighborhood house.

This student recognizes that learning language is not simply a matter of acquiring a set of facts about a language and applying them, and suggests that the support that people need is inherent to the cognitive and social complexity of the task, rather than a sign of deficit or weakness on the part of the learner. Evoking our reading of Deborah Brandt's *Literacy in American Lives*, the student recognizes the layered nature of personal history, with language, literacy, and emotions that shape the present learning situation.

We see that kind of awareness also among my colleague's students writing in Spanish:

> Yo aprendí de las luchas de los estudiantes trabajando con migo y de los estudiantes que estaban aprendiendo. Mis compañeros me abrieron los ojos de ver la realidad que la barrera de idioma que existe para los estudiantes de ESOL también existe para muchos americanos que solamente hablan un idioma y que hay un paralelo: sin la capacidad de comunicarse a veces se sienten sin poder.

Whether or not language and literacy practices were made explicit in course content, then, the experience of working in the ESOL course foregrounded the disconnect between status and English-language proficiency, and the possibility of language performance to garner enormous power.

The second category that I discovered is students' engagement with translingual practice, or working creatively across languages to create meaning. Because my students didn't generally speak much Spanish, they needed accommodation from the Spanish-speaking college students who moved more easily between the two worlds. Their English monolingualism, while giving them special status in the broader U.S. economy,[5] put them in a deficit in our specially devised speech community. But in the reflections, the English monolingual students displayed a remarkable flexibility with communication. Perhaps it was by *not* having Spanish at the tips of their tongues that their communicative creativity blossomed. For example,

> I realized that talking isn't the only way of communicating. During the time at Neighborhood House, communication was in English, Spanish and sometimes even through pictures and facial expressions. The little Spanish I knew proved to be assistance in communication but sometimes honestly my Spanish and my ESOL student Linda's English weren't enough to help us other understand each other all the time. The language difference allowed for a door to be open which allowed me to learn Spanish from them as I help them learn English.

I was touched to see this student still grappling with the metaphor of the language barrier that we had puzzled over in class. By the time he was writing his final reflection essay, this student has totally erased the idea of the wall: now, a language is a door that can be opened and closed. When it is open, meaning can pass through in *any* language. The student has transcended his monolingual assumptions, the ones that most of us inherit: that one speaks only in one language or another; that full fluency is the optimal state for communication; that teacher passes knowledge on to learner. Several students described how their English monolingualism became more obvious when it came time to do the oral history project, and yet the same students described a feeling like this one:

> My interviewee felt more comfortable speaking Spanish the entire interview. Being a monolingual student myself, I was unable to hear his story until it was later translated for me. Although I did not get to hear the story from him first hand, as I was reading the transcript I felt as if I knew what he had been saying all along.

This student's idea that "I knew what he was saying all along" is idealistic, perhaps, at least in a literal sense: he could not have translated what his oral history partner was saying. If it were a proficiency test, he would have failed it. However, his feeling speaks to the underlying spirit of the translingual approach, a feeling that fundamentally we are communicating out of our shared humanity, and that we all have equal access to language and to truth.

What I think is emerging in these student reflections, then, is a more sophisticated view of language, moving from the simple idea of language as a school subject or a self-evident marker of cultural identity to a complex idea of language and literacy as emerging from history, involving layers of personal experience, and most significantly, existing within communities, rather than within individuals. Language is not a thing that is contained within the brain of one person: it exists *only* when people use it to communicate, in semantic, symbolic, even bodily ways. That notion has profound significance when we consider the ethical implications of community-based learning and community literacy work.

Conclusions

When students and community partners have the opportunity to learn together, whether that learning is happening around the acquisition of Spanish or English, or learning about the immigrant experience or creating written texts together, they can begin to acquire a metalinguistic awareness of what language is, how it works, and how it can be theirs to use and enjoy. Elise refers often to the notion of *confianza*, a kind of interpersonal trust and understanding that can't easily be translated to English. *Confianza* allows learning and collaboration to take place; in my mind, it allows for linguistic creativity. Without it, the literacy community that we set up, where no two people share exactly the same language and literacy history, would not have been possible.

I am not suggesting that notions of language proficiency will not be with us, in ways that will be defended as useful and necessary, for a long time to come.[6] However, if we put proficiency concerns first, community literacy would never be possible. Proficiency keeps us working in what Goldblatt calls a "throughput" model of educational work, in which "[w]e move students along a path marked by diplomas and certificates, occupy them with reading and writing tasks, determine their achievements with tests or papers" (315). Community students who come to the ESOL class have hopes for increased English-language proficiency that parallel the college students' desires for the valuable credential of service learning. However, within the translingual setting itself, the proficiency model may be set aside. No one is getting graded; no one will take a test at the end. The goal is to communicate, to create texts together. What we accomplished was memorable: students seemed to become more flexible, open, courageous participants in a community endeavor to learn language. In collaboration with the community students, they created written texts that will be saved and reread. They began to understand that commonplaces about the need for immigrants to learn English are driven as much by ideologies—changeable ones—as by apparently practical need. And they put language in a broader understanding of literacy sponsorship (Brandt 2001, 17-22) and the mechanisms that welcome some of us in to full membership in democracy while leaving others out. As teachers, we can aid the process of becoming translingual not through indoctrination but through careful planning and collaboration, an openness to student attitudes towards language, and a conviction that communication takes place across boundaries every day. I am all the more convinced that a translingual approach to communication will go a long ways in the broader work of the community literacy, showing us in real, literal terms how we can create meaning and make things happen across a range of settings and languages, even those far from the centers of English.

Endnotes

1. "The concept of language as a rigid, monolithic structure is false, even if it has proved to be a useful fiction in the development of linguistics." Einar Ingvald Haugen, *The Ecology of Language* (Stanford: Stanford University Press, 1972), 325. See also Canagarajah 2007.

2. As an approach, translingualism has developed in research areas such as global Englishes (Pennycook, Blommaert, Canagarajah), education (García and Kleifgen, Jerskey), and applied linguistics and TESOL (Silva and Matsuda, Pavlenko, Fernández Dobao). It is gaining rapid recognition in rhetoric and composition (Donahue; Horner, Lu, and Matsuda, eds. 2010; Horner, Lu, Royster, and Trimbur 2011; Horner, NeCamp, and Donahue 2011; Canagarajah ed. 2013).

3. See especially Horner, Jones, Royster, and Trimbur, as well as Horner, NeCamp, and Donahue

4. See Macintosh

5. See Kramsch.

6. See especially Atkinson et al.

Works Cited

Anzaldúa, Gloria. "How to Tame a Wild Tongue." In *Ways of Reading: An Anthology for Writers*, edited by David Bartholomae and Anthony Petroskey. Ninth. Boston: Bedford/St. Martin's, 2010.

Atkinson, Dwight et al. "Clarifying the Relationship Between L2 Writing and Translingual Writing: An Open Letter to Writing Studies Editors and Organization Leaders." *College English* 77.4 (2015): 383–386. Print.

Blommaert, Jan. *The Sociolinguistics of Globalization. Cambridge Approaches to Language Contact.* Cambridge, UK ; New York: Cambridge University Press, 2010.

Brandt, Deborah. *Literacy in American Lives.* Cambridge ; New York: Cambridge University Press, 2001.

Canagarajah, A. Suresh. "Introduction." In *Literacy as Translingual Practice: Between Communities and Classrooms*, 1–10. New York: Routledge, 2013.

———. , ed. *Literacy as Translingual Practice: Between Communities and Classrooms.* New York: Routledge, 2013.

———. "Shifting the Paradigm: Towards a Translingual Rhetoric of Writing." presented at the 5th Biennial RSA Summer Institute, Lawrence, KS, June 8, 2013.

Canagarajah, Suresh. "After Disinvention: Possibilities for Communication, Community and Competence." In *Disinventing and Reconstituting Languages*, edited by Sinfree (ed. and introd.) Makoni, Alastair (ed. and introd.) Pennycook, and Ofelia (foreword) García, 233–239. Bilingual Education and Bilingualism (Bilingual Education and Bilingualism): 62. Clevedon, England: Multilingual Matters, 2007.

———. "Lingua Franca English, Multilingual Communities, and Language Acquisition." *The Modern Language Journal* 91, no. s1 (2007): 923–939.

Donahue, Christiane. "'Internationalization' and Composition Studies" Reorienting the Discourse." *College Composition and Communication* 61, no. 2 (2009): 212–234.

Fernández Dobao, Ana. "Collaborative Writing Tasks in the L2 Classroom: Comparing Group, Pair, and Individual Work." *Journal of Second Language Writing* 21, no. 1 (March 2012): 40–58.

Firth, Alan. "The Discursive Accomplishment of Normality: On 'lingua franca'English and Conversation Analysis." *Journal of Pragmatics* 26, no. 2 (1996): 237–259.

García, Ofelia, and Hugo Baetens Beardsmore. *Bilingual Education in the 21st Century: A Global Perspective*. Malden, MA; Oxford: Wiley-Blackwell Pub., 2009.

García, Ofelia, and Jo Anne Kleifgen. *Educating Emergent Bilinguals: Policies, Programs, and Practices for English Language Learners*. New York: Teachers College Press, 2010.

Goldblatt, Eli. "Alinsky's Reveille." In *Writing and Community Engagement: A Critical Sourcebook*, edited by Thomas Deans, Barbara Roswell, and Adrian J. Wurr. Boston: Bedford/St. Martin's, 2010. 313-334.

Haugen, Einar Ingvald. *The Ecology of Language*. Stanford University Press, 1972.

Horner, Bruce, Min-Zhan Lu, and Paul Kei Matsuda, eds. *Cross-Language Relations in Composition*. Carbondale: Southern Illinois University Press, 2010.

Horner, Bruce, Min-Zhan Lu, Jacqueline Jones Royster, and John Trimbur. "Language Difference in Writing: Toward a Translingual Approach." *College English* 73, no. 3 (2011): 303–321.

Horner, Bruce, Samantha NeCamp, and Christiane Donahue. "Toward a Multilingual Composition Scholarship: From English Only to a Translingual Norm." *College Composition and Communication* 63, no. 2 (2011): 269–300.

Jerskey, Maria. "Literacy Brokers in the Contact Zone, Year 1: The Crowded Safe House." In *Literacy as Translingual Practice: Between Communities and Classrooms*, edited by A. Suresh Canagarajah, 197–206. New York: Routledge, 2013.

Kramsch, Claire. "The Privilege of the Nonnative Speaker." In *The Sociolinguistics of Foreign-Language Classrooms: Contributions of the Native, the Near-Native, and the Non-Native Speaker*, edited by Carl (ed. and introd.) Blyth, 251–262. Issues in Language Program Direction: A Series of Annual Volumes by the AAUSC (ILPD). Boston, MA: Thomson Heinle, 2003.

"Literacy as Translingual Practice: Between Communities and Classrooms (Paperback) - Routledge." Accessed April 4, 2013.

McIntosh, Peggy. "Unpacking the Invisible Knapsack." In *White Privilege: Essential Readings on the Other Side of Racism*, edited by Paula S. Rothenberg, 121–125. 4th ed. New York: Worth Publishers, 2012.

Pavlenko, Aneta. "Switching Languages: Translingual Writers Reflect on Their Craft." *International Journal of Bilingual Education and Bilingualism* 8, no. 4 (2005): 345–352.

Pennycook, Alastair. "English As A Language Always In Translation." *European Journal of English Studies* 12, no. 1 (April 2008): 33–47.

———. "Translingual English." *Australian Review of Applied Linguistics* 31, no. 3 (December 2008): 30.

Silva, Tony (ed. and introd.), and Paul Kei Matsuda, eds. *Practicing Theory in Second Language Writing*. West Lafayette, Ind: Parlor Press, 2010.

Swain, Merrill. "'New' Mainstream SLA Theory: Expanded and Enriched." *The Modern Language Journal* 91, no. 5 (2007): 820–836. doi:10.1111/j.0026-7902.2007.00671.x.

Trimbur, John. "Linguistic Memory and the Uneasy Settlement of U.S. English." In *Cross-Language Relations in Composition*, edited by Bruce (ed. and introd.) Horner, Min-Zhan (ed.) Lu, and Paul Kei (ed.) Matsuda, 21–41. Carbondale, IL: Southern Illinois UP, 2010.

Zentella, Ana Celia. *Building on Strength: Language and Literacy in Latino Families and Communities*. New York; Covina, Calif.: Teachers College Press ; California Association for Bilingual Education, 2005.

Author Bio

Elizabeth Kimball teaches writing and linguistics, and directs the College Writing Program, at Drew University in Madison, NJ. She is also involved in community-based learning projects with local Latino/a communities. Her research focuses on language and learning in communities, past and present. She is published in *Rhetoric Review and Reflections: A Journal of Public Rhetoric, Civic Writing, and Service Learning*. She would like to thank the staff and volunteer teachers of the Morristown Neighborhood House, especially Rosa Chilquillo, and Elise DuBord, now of the University of Northern Iowa.

Book and New Media Reviews

Saul Hernandez and Anthony D. Boynton, II, Interns
Georgia College and State University

From the Book & New Media Review Editor's Desk
Jessica Shumake
Georgia College and State University

While attending a Saturday workshop at my university on how communities can build strong and sustainable relationships with universities that serve the public good, I heard a powerful ecological metaphor from a community leader who represents the Collins P. Lee Harrisburg Community Center and Garden. This community leader, from a high-need area in middle Georgia that was devastated economically with the loss of thousands of state jobs, articulated a method for sharing with her neighbors the lost art of growing one's own food. Community Garden volunteers recently built raised beds for edible plants through a Knight Foundation Grant. The plan of action to share this development with the community included harvesting seedlings, planting them in Dixie cups, and going door to door to give residents a seedling and instructions on how to care for the plant. One resident, who recently contributed her talents to a large mural on the Harrisburg Center's exterior walls, expressed that she believes inviting residents to cultivate garden plots is an ecological approach to community building.

Janine Morris's keyword essay on *ecology* establishes the tone for the reviews in this issue by examining the ecological metaphors that frame community building efforts and literacy work. Morris' essay further explores rhetorical models and networked views on literacy environments, digital technologies, and educational practices. In his review of *After the Public Turn: Composition, Counterpublics, and the Citizen Bricoleur*, Jason Luther examines the discursive resources of maker culture and how its DIY ethos can be applied to the composition classroom to offer students opportunities to make cultural interventions from resources that are ready at hand. In Cynthia Delaney's review of Elaine B. Richardson's *How Education Saved My Life*, it becomes apparent that for Richardson individuals are first and foremost individuals-in-communities. Delaney's review articulates why an asset-based framework is required to gain a deeper understanding of the complex pathways Richardson navigated to earn her doctorate.

Anne-Marie Hall's review of *Del Otro Lado* examines how Susan V. Meyers traces the relationship between social networks, migration, literacy, and economic status to investigate how literacy institutions can be deflected and accessed for the ends of self-preservation. Hall's review foregrounds what Meyers terms the "rhetorical stance" that the rural Mexican community members she spent a year with had toward literacy. Community members were strategic in the ways they put into practice the aspects of literacy education that worked for them and discarded the rest. Hall articulates that there is an urgent need for educators to become more responsive to students' emerging, transnational, and diverse literacy practices. Educators' responsiveness to multiple literacies is especially pressing given that educators themselves create literacy crises when they fail to "understand how the disconnect between the curriculum and the values it imparts do not address the communities' real needs" or they undervalue the funds of knowledge students contribute to classrooms.

Jessica E. Slentz's review of *New Media Literacies and Participatory Cultures Across Borders* articulates that popular culture on a global scale is this cohesive collection's point of convergence. Slentz recommends the edited collection to community literacy practitioners and theorists as a "comprehensive resource on adolescent literacy practices online" and a nuanced exploration of the ways people co-construct identity and meaning through digital technologies and multimodal literacy practices. Angela Clark-Oates likewise recommends Jill McCracken's *Street Sex Worker's Discourse: Realizing Material Change through Agential Choice* for researchers and practitioners interested in rhetorical agency within communities that are differentially empowered and diminished by normative discourses, ideologies, and cultural practices.

Ecology

Janine Morris
University of Cincinnati

Keyword Essay

Within community literacy scholarship, ecological perspectives are used to characterize the literacy and language practices of various groups. Director of the Lancaster Literacy Research Centre, David Barton draws from biology to theorize ecology as the study of "the interrelationship of an area of human activity and its environment. It is concerned with how the activity—literacy in this case—is part of the environment and at the same time influences and is influenced by the environment" (29). The reciprocal nature of ecologies, and the way they account for the distribution, influence, and movement of organisms within and between environments makes ecology an ideal term for characterizing the relationships among groups, technologies, and cultures that influence the ways individuals learn, communicate, and interact with one another. In this keyword essay, I will highlight the appropriateness of ecology for describing networked communication and literacy practices, as well as offer an overview of how compositionists and community literacy practitioners have used ecological approaches in the work they do.

It is necessary here to distinguish an ecological approach from one that is exclusively environmental. In 1989, environmentalist David Orr defined ecological literacy as "the demanding capacity to distinguish between health and disease in natural systems and to understand their relation to health and disease in human ones; knowledge of this sort is best acquired out of doors" (334). Ecological literacy in this respect is concerned with reading the natural environment. Orr's call for increased environmental awareness and attention to the ways humans impact environments remains increasingly urgent. However, this keyword essay focuses instead on how scholars and practitioners have adopted ecological metaphors to characterize literacy environments. The ecological approach I examine aligns more closely with that of ecocomposition theories than those of the ecological literacy Orr defines. In their *Natural Discourse: Toward Ecocomposition*, Sid Dobrin and Christian Weisser define ecocomposition as "the study of the relationships between environments (and by that we mean natural, constructed, and even imagined places) and discourse (seeking, writing, and thinking)" (6). Dobrin and Weisser's approach does not exclude environmental concerns but instead makes the role of language and discourse central in making those concerns visible. As Rhonda Davis suggests in her discussion of ecocomposition and community literacy, "while ecological literacy and the pedagogical approaches that result do not focus exclusively on environmental concerns, they have the potential to expand participants' awareness of such concerns" (80).

Literacy and Composing Ecologies

Before turning to ways that community literacy practitioners have used ecologies to explain the work they do, it is important to understand how ecologies have come to characterize writing environments and literacy practices. Margaret Syverson's *The Wealth of Reality: An Ecology of Composition* provides a theoretical framework for studying composing processes by situating them within ecological systems. Using biological and cognitive theories, Syverson explains how concepts of distribution, emergence, embodiment, and enaction appear in writing environments and complicate our understanding of how writers compose. Syverson's definition of writing ecologies extends beyond those of writers like Marilyn Cooper, whose approach to ecologies, according to Syverson, "is rather sketchy and limited to social interactions via ideas, purposes, interpersonal interactions, cultural norms, and textual forms" (24). Instead, Syverson's definition of composing ecologies is grounded in multidisciplinary theories of complex systems, which involve a "network of independent agents—people, atoms, neurons, or molecules, for instance—[who] act and interact in parallel with each other, simultaneously reacting to and co-constructing their own environment" (3). To ground this theory, Syverson draws from biology and physics, while also looking to cognitive science, communications, philosophy, and economics (2). Adopting Syverson's ecological approach requires theorists to "take into account the complex interrelationships in which the writing is embedded; the people and texts that form a larger conversation in which the writer, text, and reader participate and from which the 'ideas' emerge to take written shape" (6). This expanded understanding of the writing process goes beyond looking at the writer, text, and composing situation as discrete elements and requires a more integrated and networked view of writing.

Because Syverson's approach accounts for multiple components of a writing situation, including psychological, material, social, and cognitive dimensions of writing, her view of composition ecologies is useful for understanding the larger structures that surround writing environments. Syverson uses case studies of writers and readers to examine diverse sites of composing in her manuscript, looking to Charles Reznikoff's autobiographical poetry, a composition classroom, and a Gulf War computer forum made up of scientists. These varied examples are important to community literacy practitioners as they highlight how malleable Syverson's ecological theorizations are to numerous sites of analysis.

While Syverson outlines a multifaceted approach to understanding writing, other theorists have used ecological perspectives to characterize literacy development. For instance, Kirsten Kainz and Lynne Vernon-Feagans examine the sociocultural influences on reading development with a cohort of "economically disadvantaged children" (407); while Gutiérrez et al. study the polylingual learning ecologies of children's linguistic repertoires. David Barton's 1994 *Literacy: An Introduction to the Ecology of Written Language* uses an ecological metaphor to define and explain the multiple social and linguistic factors involved in literacy development. Seeing literacy as a set of "social practices associated with particular symbol systems and their related technologies," Barton draws on an ecological metaphor to develop his integrated view of literacy learning (32). Barton suggests that "rather than isolating literacy activities from everything else in order to understand them, an ecological approach aims to understand how literacy is embedded in other human activity, its embeddedness in social life and in thought, and its position in history, language and learning" (32). Barton's text is characterized as an introductory approach to the field of literacy and examines literacy acquisition beyond educational practices from both local and global perspectives, focusing on child and adult print literacy acquisition, language development, and multilingual literacy practices.

Ecological Approaches to Community Literacy

Recent community literacy scholarship has argued for the importance of practitioners to adopt an ecopedagogical stance. Rhonda Davis examines the connections between ecopedagogy and community literacy in her 2013 article "A Place for Ecopedagogy in Community Literacy," demonstrating how "literacy as an ecological act delves into the ways compositionists and community literacy practitioners see themselves in relation to the world and the positive potential of holding such a view" (79). Davis' ecopedagogy centers on local concerns and community building by "plac[ing] ecoliteracy at the center and oppos[ing] the globalization of ideologies such as neoliberalism and imperialism that may hinder local literacy efforts" (78). Such a framework requires local, expert, and societal knowledge in order to better assess and find solutions for particular community needs. Davis draws from critical pedagogy and ecoliteracy in order to "guide teachers and practitioners of all types not only to see the collective potential of human beings, but to develop an appreciation for it and foster social justice" (78). Her article applies ecopedagogy to Lorraine Higgins, Elenore Long, and Linda Flower's rhetorical model of community literacy as a way to showcase its applicability for community literacy practitioners. Ultimately, Davis aims to showcase how "ecopedagogy is a unique and powerful pedagogical strategy in which to frame an approach to service learning programs and other activities engaged in the goals of community literacy" (83). Encouraging a reflective pedagogy that recognizes the impact of various relationships is echoed through the community literacy work focusing on ecologies.

While Davis argues for community literacy practitioners to adopt an ecological approach more broadly, much of the scholarship in community literacy uses ecological metaphors to account for the literacy practices of particular groups. For instance, Martin Paviour-Smith uses an ecological metaphor to examine the home-based language acquisition practices of a community in the Republic of Vanuatu. Using an ethnographic approach, Paviour-Smith traces the use of English, French, Bislama, and Aulua in different contexts to explore vernacular literacies and language dominance. In another article, Lynn Mario T. Menezes de Souza discusses multimodal writing practices of members of the Kashinawà community in Brazil. To avoid the privileging of alphabetic texts over the visual texts produced by community members, he proposes "the need for a reappraisal of the status of local indigenous knowledges and their interaction with what are considered to be nonlocal (universal?) theories of literacy and writing on which policies of indigenous education may be unsuspectingly, and therefore, uncritically based" (262). Both Paviour-Smith and de Souza account for the larger material and sociocultural dimensions of the communities they examine in order to explore localized language use and visual writing practices that value indigenous forms of meaning making.

Further examples of community research present themselves in an ecological themed volume of *The Encyclopedia of Language and Education*. In the "Introduction to Volume 9: Ecology of Language," Angela Creese and Peter Martin open this edited collection by focusing on how contributors explore the local and situated networks of the groups they study. An ecological perspective for Creese and Martin offers a framework for describing and deconstructing the relationships between speakers and the languages and literacies that make up their lives. They define language ecology as "the study of diversity within specific sociopolitical settings," challenging hierarchies and hegemonies located in "perceived natural language orders" (xii-xiv). Thus, the study of language ecologies takes on an unruly tone, disrupting normalized structures and calling into question organizing hierarchies. While the focus of the larger volume is to examine theoretical debates within language ecologies in more detail, the sections of interest to community literacy practitioners are those that disrupt the relationships between individuals and literacy practices in particular situations. For example, Sandra Kipp examines multilingual history and language preservation in Australia; Angela Creese and Peter Martin explore Gujarati language practices in community schools in England; Angel M.Y. Lin analyses the hybrid writing practices of Cantonese speakers in Hong Kong; and Kate Pahl questions the social relationships present in various home, education, and community discourses.

Within Creese and Martin's collection is Karin Tusting's review essay, "Ecologies of New Literacies: Implications for Education," which chronicles new literacy research beginning in the mid-1990s. Tusting's aim in the article is to describe "an ecological perspective on new literacies, which studies how changing literacy practices are intimately associated with networks of changing social practices and technologies, from local to global levels" (317). The ecological view that Tusting forwards is one that sees a reciprocal relationship between the emergence of new literacies and their contexts of use. Within new literacy studies, Tusting examines how learning practices and environments change with the addition of multimodal technologies. Tusting reviews research looking at the influences of new literacies in a number of contexts including Richard Lanham's and Nancy Kaplan's research on the emergence of 'e-literacies' in the 1990s; Jackie Marsh's research on young children's exposure to popular culture, multimedia, and digital technologies in home environments; James Gee and Beth Cross' work on video game learning and players; as well as Bill Cope and Mary Kalantzis' global and multicultural analyses of multimodal teaching, to name a few of the texts she examines. Ultimately, Tusting suggests that further research into the role of insiders and outsiders in new literacy studies is needed, as we see shifting perspectives between young "technological 'insiders'" and those of the generations before them (327).

Within new literacies, Syverson's ecological theorizations gain scholarly ground. In a 2008 *Literacy* article, she applies her ecological model of distribution, emergence, embodiment, and enaction to literacy learning more specifically, as this model "takes into account the complex ecosystems within which teachers and learners learn, adapt, interact, communicate, and connect" (109). Stating that a linear and sequential view of literacy learning is insufficient to account for the way individuals learn in increasingly technological environments, Syverson offers an ecological approach that goes beyond a focus on the individual to account for the complex systems of networks that are constantly in flux. Because literacy learning increasingly takes place in technological environments, which Syverson suggests are characterized by "randomness and spontaneity, not predictability; by diversity and plurality, not standardization; and by uncertainty, not certainty," this literacy learning landscape calls for an ecological approach that considers "connections, relationships, flows, and dynamics of change over time" (110). Syverson uses the Learning Record, which looks at a multitude of data from numerous contexts to determine how and what individuals are learning, as an alternative framework to better understand the complexities of literacy learning (112-14). While a model like the Learning Record has limitations which Syverson addresses, this framework is one that is more apt to account for the complexities involved in literacy learning in networked environments.

Ecological metaphors have played an important role allowing community literacy practitioners and theorists to more closely examine various environments where reading, writing, and language development take place. Ecological views take into account the individual, environmental, material, and sociocultural factors that influence learning outcomes in a number of situations and recognize the impact and disruptive potential of multiple variables in such environments. The research cited in this essay showcases a myriad of approaches to ecological metaphors that theorists and practitioners have adopted to account for the literacy practices in the environments they study.

Works Cited

Barton, David. *Literacy: An Introduction to the Ecology of Written Language*. Oxford, UK: Blackwell Publishers, 1994. Print.

Cope, Bill and Mary Kalantzis. *Multiliteracies: Literacy Learning and the Design of Social Futures*. New York: Routledge, 2000. Print.

Creese, Angela and Peter Martin. "Introduction to Volume 9: The Ecology of Language." *Encyclopedia of Language and Education*; Volume 9: Ecology of Language. Ed. Angela Creese, Peter Martin, and Nancy Hornberger. New York: Springer Science & Business Media LLC, 2008. xiii-xviii. Print.

Cross, Beth. "Split Frame Thinking and Multiple Scenario Awareness: How Boys' Game Expertise Reshapes Possible Structures of Sense in a Digital World." *Discourse: Studies in the Cultural Politics of Education* 26.3 (2005): 333-53. Print.

Davis, Rhonda. "A Place for Ecopedagogy in Community Literacy." *Community Literacy Journal* 7.2 (Spring 2013): 77-91. Print.

de Souza, Lynn Mario T. Menezes. "A Case Among Cases, A World Among Worlds: The Ecology of Writing Among the Kashinawá in Brazil." *Journal of Language, Identity, and Education* 1.4 (2002): 261-78. Print.

Dobrin, Sidney and Christian Weisser. *Natural Discourse: Toward Ecocomposition.* Albany, NY: State U. of New York P., 2002. Print.

Gee, James. *What Videos Games Have to Teach Us About Learning and Literacy.* New York: Palgrave MacMillan, 2003. Print.

Gutiérrrez, Kris D., et al. "Polylingual and Polycultural Learning Ecologies: Mediating Emergent Academic Literacies for Dual Language Learners." *Journal of Early Childhood Literacy* 11.2 (2011): 232-61. Print.

Higgins, Lorraine, Elenore Long, and Linda Flower. "Community Literacy: A Rhetorical Model for Personal and Public Inquiry." *Community Literacy Journal* 1.1 (2006): 9-43. Print.

Kains, Kirsten and Lynne Vernon-Feagans. "The Ecology of Early Reading Development for Children in Poverty." *The Elementary School Journal* 107.5 (2007): 407-27. Print.

Kaplan, Nancy. "E-Literacies: Politics, Hypertext, and Other Cultural Formations in the Age of Print." *Computer-Mediated Communication Magazine* 2.3 (1995): 3. Print.

Kipp, Sandra. "The Language Ecology of Australia's Community Languages." *Encyclopedia of Language and Education; Volume 9: Ecology of Language.* Ed. Angela Creese, Peter Martin, and Nancy Hornberger. New York: Springer Science &Business Media LLC, 2008. 69-84. Print.

Lanham, Richard. "Digital Literacy." *Scientific American* 237.3 (1995): 253-355. Print.

Lin, Angel M.Y. "The Ecology of Literacy in Hong Kong." *Encyclopedia of Language and Education; Volume 9: Ecology of Language.* Ed. Angela Creese, Peter Martin, and Nancy Hornberger. New York: Springer Science & Business Media LLC, 2008. 291-303. Print.

Marsh, Jackie, ed. Popular Culture, *New Media and Digital Literacy in Early Childhood.* New York: Routledge, 2005. Print.

Orr, David W. "Ecological Literacy." *Conservation Biology* 3.4 (December 1989): 334-35. Print.

Pahl, Kate. "The Ecology of Literacy and Language: Discourses, Identities, and Practices in Homes, Schools, and Communities." *Encyclopedia of Language and Education; Volume 9: Ecology of Language.* Ed. Angela Creese, Peter Martin, and Nancy Hornberger. New York: Springer Science & Business Media LLC, 2008. 305-16. Print.

Paviour-Smith, Martin. "After the Letters? The Ecology of Literacy in Aulua, Vanuatu." *New Zealand Studies in Applied Linguistics* 14.1 (2008): 1-18. Print.

Syverson, Margaret. "An Ecological View of Literacy Learning." *Literacy* 42.2 (July 2008): 109-17. Print.

———. *The Wealth of Reality: An Ecology of Composition*. Carbondale, IL: Southern Illinois UP, 1999. Print.

Tusting, Karin. "Ecologies of New Literacies: Implications for Education." *Encyclopedia of Language and Education; Volume 9: Ecology of Language*. Ed. Angela Creese, Peter Martin, and Nancy Hornberger. New York: Springer Science & Business Media LLC, 2008. 317-30. Print.

After the Public Turn: Composition, Counterpublics, and the Citizen Bricoleur

Frank Farmer
Boulder: Utah State UP, 2013. 180 pp.

Reviewed by Jason Luther
Syracuse University

As *College English*'s recent special issue on the social turn can attest, English studies in general and composition studies in particular have often embraced the epochal language of "the turn" to gauge its self-efficacy, often hinging on the mission of its determined publics and/ or the liberal mission of the university. It is in this context that Frank Farmer's book, *After the Public Turn: Composition, Counterpublics, and the Citizen Bricoleur*, is welcome, as it attempts to put these turns into perspective by splicing the concept of counterpublics into our understanding of two publics often evoked in composition studies: one cultural and ad hoc, one disciplinary and institutional.

In the introduction, Farmer begins by helpfully historicizing these various turns, winnowing in on the turn toward the public, which he explicates via Mathieu, Welch, Flower, Long, and others, while at the same time reminding us that this turn "encompasses a variety of concerns—pedagogical, institutional, disciplinary, and cultural" (24). Yet, for all of the public turn's complexity, Farmer argues that "definitional ambiguity" and traditional attachments to public sphere theory have led us to largely ignore *counterpublics*, a term he traces from Negt and Kluge to Nancy Fraser, the latter proposes that they exist in order to circulate counter-discourses that permit oppositional identities (16). Farmer also spends a significant portion of the introduction with Michael Warner's *Publics and Counterpublics*, which challenges Habermas and Fraser's ideas that counterpublics and its discourses must be deliberative. Importantly for composition studies, Warner proposes that counterpublic discourse can be affective, expressive and otherwise, non-rational. This should interest composition studies, says Farmer, because it opens up our students *and ourselves* to alternative, bottom-up versions of citizenship, democratic participation, and public engagement—understandings that include an array of discourses, forms and sites for social change and rebuke the impulse to look to canonized public intellectuals, politicians, and social policy experts.

Chapter one is the first of two chapters on cultural publics and centers on zine culture, specifically anarchist and punk zines. Farmer's method is theoretical and historical in this chapter, using deCerteau, Levi-Strauss, and Hebdige to help explore the term *bricolage*, or "the artful 'making do' of the 'handyman' who, using only those materials and tools readily available to him, constructs new objects out of worn ones, who imagines new uses for what has been cast aside, discarded" (31). Farmer argues that because the practice of bricolage is "simultaneously resistant and constructive" it is useful for reimagining democracy through the *citizen bricoleur*, "an intellectual activist of the unsung sort, thoroughly committed to, and implicated in, the task of understanding how publics are made, unmade, remade, and better made, often from little more than the discarded scraps of earlier attempts—constructions that, for whatever reason, are no longer legitimate or serviceable" (36). Punk zine authors embody this citizen, since its culture articulates an explicit DIY ethos, the terms of which are laid out by Farmer at the end of the chapter. Such an ethic denies print's exclusivity and assigns making from remnant materials, rather than the consumption of new ones, the constitutive feature of its discourse. In this way, zine culture is able to "transform ordinary consumption into an alternative kind of production" (53).

Chapter two pushes this idea further by reintroducing zines as an exemplary cultural public, "a social formation, established primarily through texts, whose constructed identity functions, in some measure, to oppose and critique the accepted norms of the society in which it emerges" (56). He borrows heavily from Warner in this chapter as he looks to zines as cultural publics to demonstrate the kind of "poetic world-making" through reflexive circulation inherent to the counterpublics Warner observes in his work. That is, Farmer uses zines as "the quintessential example" (66) of a way to show how citizen *bricoleurs* can use various forms—as opposed to the content-driven arenas of deliberative rhetoric or rational-critical debate—to contest the dominant discourses of publics. As a result of these forms, new "spaces of circulation" are created that have transformative effects, requiring "a different sense of what agency might mean when it comes to counterpublic discourse and the worlds they make" (62). Zines, then, become an illustrative site for understanding the "discursive resources" necessary for the development of counterpublics—a site where "publicness assumes a far greater emphasis than it ordinarily does", where discourse is a way of being, not simply a space for deliberation and decision-making (66-67).

A key moment in this chapter sees Farmer looking at zines in the context of the digital age. While Farmer rightly acknowledges that contemporary DIY print culture makes use of both print and online forms of making, the social function of zines rests upon the affordances of their materiality; more specifically, zines offer intimacy for feminist and queer communities by offering archival traces to make counterhistories. This leads Farmer to wonder if a DIY ethos, as he has imagined it, can even exist on the Web. This question is important if, as Warner and Farmer argue, counterpublics exist as ways of being, not simply as deliberative discourses. Blogs and other forms of push-button publishing, for example, make use of templates that not only restrict the capacity for world making, but also require expensive and often incorporated infrastructure. This question is also important for community publishers who must consider the costs—both literal and figurative—of choose certain sponsors of circulation, whether they might be local institutions or multinational corporations like Facebook.

Farmer ends the chapter considering the effect zines might have in the composition classroom. Specifically, he considers how a DIY ethos defines "rhetorical success" by the extent to which one maker inspires another; he recommends we invite our students to make this their rhetorical goal through self-publication. Moreover, by asking them to tend to issues of format, we can "teach students about visual and typographical rhetoric" (Farmer 86). And perhaps most importantly, Farmer asks us to consider our classrooms as DIY projects instead of "by others, for others," a critique of the textbook-centered classroom that grafts hyper-professionalization onto our students. Finally, Farmer considers how the process of zine-making—through finding materials, designing layouts, imagining readers, engaging production methods, and circulating copies—dovetails with a version citizenship that can "transform consumption into alternate forms of production" (89).

Farmer then turns to academic or disciplinary publics in chapters three and four, exploring what it means when academics "go public" beyond the their traditional roles as public intellectuals, experts, or activists. In Chapter three, he searches for an alternative role through three counterpublic expressions plucked from the literature of architecture, via Shannon Mattern; teacher education, via Henry Gioux and Peter McLaren; and science and technology studies, via David Hess. Through these three case studies, Farmer describes the nature, activities, and extent of various disciplinary counterpublics, arriving at three possible forms: Internal, Autonomous, and Rhetorical. Internal Disciplinary Counterpublics are Janus-faced, projecting disciplinary conversations outward by cooperating with more traditional counterpublics in a manner unsanctioned by the disciplines themselves; Autonomous Disciplinary Counterpublics are counterpublics in and of themselves, such as departments of gender studies; finally, Rhetorical Disciplinary Counterpublics are built from discourses and networks. This last version importantly tables reified social formations to consider the rhetorical activities of *all* disciplines that are capable of creating what Eric Doxtader calls *counterpublicity* (126).

In chapter four, Farmer considers the bad press of composition—the countless op-eds from the George Wills, Stanley Fishes, or Louis Menands, who use their status as public intellectuals—and not instructors of writing—to disparage the state of literacy and literacy instruction and in so doing exclude the very literacy professionals who are best qualified to speak. In response, Farmer asks readers to consider the potential for composition's counterpublicity by "insinuat[ing] ourselves into discourses that were never meant to include us to begin with" (138). This can be done, he argues, by exploiting an ambiguity that exists between the addressivity of audiences and publics through the arts of bricolage, which "might be the methodology best suited for all counterpublics" (148). Farmer is not terribly specific about how we might go about this, but he does suggest we embrace the ethos of the *bricoleur* and publicly abandon both the celebrity of the public intellectual and our titles as experts or activists; instead we might consider the ways in which we perform their functions as we work with and through the liminal scenes of the extracurriculum to *make* publics.

While this portion of the book might benefit from more specific examples, Farmer's larger point should not be lost on community literacy scholars who have used their "expertise situationally, creatively, tactically" (150) to make community literacy projects such as Adela Licona and Stephen Russell's *think-and-do tanks* centered around youth health and sexuality, just to give one example. That is, instead of only *responding* to public discourse when addressed (whether on our campuses or off), Farmer encourages us to consider crafting our own projects that help reimagine citizenship and the public sphere as something that goes beyond the critical and rational, that goes beyond discursive modes, in order to create publics from the materials at hand. What this may look like is in practice difficult to say, especially in frugal professional environments where *bricolage* is just another term for resourcefulness. "Do more with less" can be the mantra of the punk, but also the bureaucratic. Yet, *After the Public Turn* provides us with the language and terms necessary to distinguish between them as the field continues to consider the ways making, DIY, and counterpublics can inform not only what we think and do within our respective spheres, but also how we can actually make them.

Phd to Ph.D.: How Education Saved My Life
Elaine B. Richardson
Philadelphia: Parlor P, 2013. 264 pp.

Reviewed by Cynthia Delaney
Michigan Technological University

In *PHD (Po Ho on Dope) to Ph.D.: How Education Saved My Life*, Elaine Richardson successfully establishes a deeply personal narrative that has the potential to reach and inspire a variety of audiences both inside and outside of the academy and serves as a model of the public scholarship in the spirit of other widely influential literacy narratives, such as those by Mike Rose and Victor Villanueva. Through discussion of her own journey, Richardson's memoir is an unflinching presentation of her early life on the streets, and an unabashed celebration of literacy and education as her redemption. While literacy researchers may be hesitant of Richardson's treatment of education as a panacea (or what Harvey Graff might call the "literacy myth"), Richardson stresses the importance of "end[ing] the lie that Black people have no intellectually worthy language and literacy traditions, that English and literacy are the same across different people and cultures, and that upper class biased Whites in power and their followers (not all White people) get to define language and literacy for everyone else" (235). Richardson's argument has important implications for readers in and out of the academy by encouraging the development of a stronger examination of "teachings and mindsets that are not to our advantage" (235) and the realization, particularly for members of disadvantaged communities, that it is possible to make contributions to "culture and to the world of ideas" through challenging the paradigms and finding power in language (236).

In short, the book details Richardson's journey as a young African American female who transcends "cultural performance" and socially enforced expectations that she perform the identity of a "regla" African American girl: that is, someone who was supposed to be sexually available and readily accepting of physical abuse. Enacting this prescribed identity in her youth, Richardson's experiences with prostitution and drug addiction capture the destructive feelings of guilt and shame tied up in this identity.

As a testament to the fluidity of identity, however, Richardson also illustrates that, by means of education and the support systems (such as her mother's strength and support) on reserve for her, Richardson rewrote her sense of self within the academy, conducting research that would not only assist in her finding her voice but love for herself and self-confidence.

Beginning with her family history, Richardson establishes her roots as a good student in search of self-acceptance in the wrong places. As a preteen and teenager, she has periods of consistency in school but she lives a "double life" (periodically lending more importance to one life over the other) by simultaneously attending college and working as a prostitute, up until she is academically dismissed from Cleveland State and becomes completely immersed in "the life of street people" (110). Richardson spends a fair portion of the book discussing her history as a prostitute and details the characteristics of the men who serve as her pimps and abusers in the years before she goes back to college. Although Richardson's life falls into despair and she loses her sense of self, she realizes, after some years, having two children, and narrowly missing death several times, that she "needed to love and feel good about [herself] again" (190). When she is accepted again into Cleveland State University to finish her undergraduate degree, she "put[s her] all into school" (194) and nothing deters her from her mission to succeed as a student. In describing her years as a student and then graduate student, she places emphasis on finding her niche as a scholar and how finding her educational passion and support system drives her to continue on and receive her Ph.D.

In addition to its candor about Richardson's conflicted history, the book is notable for the lengths to which Richardson goes "to be true to the languages of her communities" (vii-viii). Richardson carefully represents the diverse voices of the people (be they pimps, boyfriends, often a combination of both) from her past. The strongest voice in the narrative is that of her mother, whose Jamaican accent Richardson captures in phonetic spellings, and who stands as a huge support system for pursuit of educational "'oppachunity'" (73) and does not abandon her through her years of addiction and prostitution. In this way, Richardson's book stays true to her communities and embodies its arguments for the importance of acknowledging and incorporating the diversity of languages that appear in classrooms and literacy workshops. As she writes, "If you don't feel good about your language or value it, you can't possibly feel good about yourself. Your language is your heart, your brain, your family, your history" (210-11).

An immersive read, the book presents Richardson engaged in conversation with readers about her personal journey through hardship and how she ultimately found self-acceptance through gaining an education and transcending self-made and societal boundaries. Accessible and poignant, Richardson's memoir would benefit undergraduate students as well as members of disadvantaged communities outside of higher education. She does not withhold details and her use of language and tone create a sense of immediacy. As she begins finding a sense of pride in herself, she realizes that there is strength in her voice as a Black woman and that she is not alone, "We weren't illiterate as the prof and tutors made us out to be. They just didn't have a clue about

Black folks. And they didn't see who we were or where we came from as an important part of the educational process" (201).

Richardson's work answers Jacqueline Jones Royster's 1996 call in "When the First Voice You Hear is Not Your Own" to strive "toward a clearer respect for human potential and achievement from whatever their source and a clearer understanding that voicing at its best is not just well-spoken but also well-heard" (40). While repeating the mantra, "Don't let them kill your voice" (207) (where "they" include unsupportive professors and an oppressive educational system) Richardson applied her life and experiences to fuel her desire and passion to complete her research on "Black language [which is most certainly] a part of African American culture" (211). Richardson's work serves as a concrete example of learning to use the power of language and narrative to create meaningful research to inspire others to follow similar paths. Because education gave her a hope and a purpose, she allowed education the power to save her life.

At first glance Richardson's bold assessment of her history is that, "where there's a will, there is always a way" (196) may seem to emphasize the individual who lifts herself up by her bootstraps. While Richardson's claim may sound naïve here, she does not blame the "will" of individuals who have not found a "way," but instead acknowledges that, through the combination of support from various systems and her "die trying" (194) attitude, she was able to achieve in her pursuit of education. Although support systems do not arise for everyone and serve everyone, Richardson's work initiates dialogue about how to remedy an unwanted life situation and strive for something greater, starting with a sense of purpose and building self-worth. In the book, Richardson marks her transition from self-loathing to the shedding of internalized shame. She notes, "I am who I am. I never wanted to put on airs and make myself out to be someone who I wasn't. I'm a girl from down the way, an ex-junkie, ex-ho, a baby mama, and I'm still just as good as anybody else on this planet" (239). Community literacy practitioners and researchers will find this book useful for examining the multiple and complex obstacles and support networks that operate to enable and constrain the sharing of stories of struggle and achievement.

Del Otro Lado: Literacy and Migration across the U.S.–Mexico Border

Susan V. Meyers
Carbondale: Southern Illinois UP, 2014. 209 pp.

Reviewed by Anne-Marie Hall
The University of Arizona

There are few researchers today in rhetoric and composition, particularly in emerging literacies, who are talking about transnational literacy practices and the effects of a changing global economy on migration and thus on literacy. In *Del Otro Lado: Literacy and Migration across the U.S.–Mexico Border*, Susan V. Meyers, a bilingual ethnographer, set a huge task for herself as she immersed herself for a full year (with a Fulbright Fellowship) in rural Mexico and then traced the migratory patterns of students in Mexico to the U.S. and back. Her reflective critical ethnography calls into question stereotypes about Mexican immigrant students—that they are lazy or disengaged or even that they are victims of a callous school system. And she shows us with insightful reasoning, passionate and personal stories, and carefully documented historical research that "migration and literacy are intimately connected—and that migration complicates and is a catalyst for literacy acquisition" (7).

Meyers argues that the *literacy contract*—what she calls that implicit and sometimes explicit understanding that literacy is a resource and if families participate, that is, subscribe, to the activities and value systems of the institution of public education, then there will be a reward. This reward is almost always supposed to be improved economic circumstances. But in rural Mexico—and I would argue in hundreds of other places in the world where there is *not* a wage-labor economy—the promise of literacy is seriously overrated. Indeed, the idea that literacy improves one's economic status is one of the greatest colonizing myths of our time as it is simply not true for most of the world. This book shows us how a local community with "few resources positions itself with respect to larger more powerful institutions" (12) that sponsor, endorse, define, and institutionalize education. While the book traces the development of this "literacy contract" in both the US and Mexico, thus setting the context for significant similarities and differences in the promise of education in both countries, it really sings when

Meyers gives voice to the people who live in the village of Villachuato, Mexico (pop. 4000), and migrate to Marshalltown, Iowa (pop. 24,000). Their voices stay with readers as they challenge much of what we *think* we know about literacy. As Meyers writes, "language is explicit; culture is not" (13). This book helps make that culture visible.

In chapter one, "Crisis and Contract: A Rhetorical Approach to Transnational Literacies," we learn about various rhetorics of crisis around literacy, tracing multiple definitions and concepts around literacy from those of the funding agency UNESCO to many in the US and in Mexico. The many sponsors of literacy include everything from religions to civic groups. Most important, Meyers makes visible the levels of awareness (implicit and explicit) that rural Mexican communities carry with respect to their life conditions and opportunities to attain resources. How these rural Mexicans position themselves socially with regards to schools is ultimately what permits them to assume what Meyers calls a more "flexible, rhetorical stance toward literacy: one that reads the implicit lines of institutions' rules and finds ways of complying, though tentatively and selectively" (36-7). And one might add "resistance" to the list of ways they respond to the threat of oppressive conditions. Remittances (both monetary and social such as values and new behaviors) brought back to Villachuato by their migrated family members do improve the social capital of the families in Villachuato, positioning "community members at home to function rhetorically, rather than reactively, to sources of social oppression" (39). In other words, there is a change, a sort of heightened awareness of the benefits and consequences of the literacy contract that the citizens of Villachuato can size up and then resist or buy into on their own terms.

In chapter two, "'Aren't You Scared?': The Changing Face of Oppression in Rural, Migrant-Sending Mexico," Meyers places herself in this community in a narrative that captures both her own personal story and sets a tone for the blending of the personal with the scholarly that permeates the ethos of the entire book. This setting of the scene shows us that the village of Villachuato is really like many communities in Mexico that send outbound migration to the US. For it is these "absent residents—what is *not* present, rather than what *is*, that truly characterizes Villachuato today" (58). In other words, this is a town that has strong community ties, ways of managing foreign influences (including a foreign researcher), and a political and economic history that is similar to others in its responses to a public education system that has not delivered on its promise in rural Mexico. Interestingly, it is through the power of fear (Aren't You Scared?) as a woman living and working alone in this isolated town that helps Meyers see how fear became a powerful force in making her, the researcher, assimilate to local behavior patterns.

In chapter three, "'They Make a Lot of Sacrifices': Foundational Rhetorics of the Mexican Education System," Meyers traces the Mexican curriculum and education system in general. Here we see how the legacies of colonialism, the strain of post-Revolutionary nation building, and the pragmatic realities coalesce in a need to "build a public education system quickly" (63). It becomes clear how the roots of the literacy contract differ in the US from Mexico. In the US, early colonists focused on building a new national consciousness that did not consider indigenous groups, while in post-

Revolutionary Mexico, the mestizo populations were firmly established and thus targeted from the beginning for education and civic engagement. This created "subtle differences in ways in which students respond to education in both settings" argues Meyers (65).

One of the unfortunate side effects of the ensuing national curriculum in Mexico is the disconnect between the curriculum and the training of teachers, all of which happens in urban areas far from the lived realities of rural communities (who do not have access to wage-labor economies). The economic realities of such a community call into question the value of a formal education—the assumptions underlying the literacy contract. Thus the endeavor of mass education—a capitalist entreaty—has little reward for rural citizens. The sacrifices they are asked to make just do not pay off or even relate to their daily lives. They are "empty promises" as Meyers puts it.

In chapter four, "'They Didn't Tell Me Anything'" Community Literacy and Resistance in Rural Mexico," Meyers delves into gender norms (and her own discomfort with these norms) in Villachuato, and it is here that we clearly see how the migratory patterns are indeed gendered in this village (men migrate, women stay back and tend the family). One thing is obvious—women have largely been left out of the scholarship on Mexican migration. Meyers goes on to show how women's "consistent form of self-preservation—whether in accessing literacy or deflecting the damaging influences of literacy institutions—was in the form of social networks" (93). This is the heart of the book, in my view—and certainly my favorite chapter. Here we see the skill of a sensitive and talented ethnographer bringing to voice six women representing four generations: Esperanza (age 99) who used letter writing to demonstrate the "power and malleability of literacy" (95); Patricia (early 70s) who parlayed her own experience with a neglectful mother and a teenage marriage into an ability to learn from returning migrants (a type of social remittance, if you will) and identified literacy as a form of power to protect her own daughter; Elvira (40 years old) whose mother would not permit her to be educated but who eventually migrated to the US for 4 years and learned much about the implications for literary, enough that her son lives permanently in the US and her daughter is one of the highest trained females in Villachuato, working for wages in a neighboring town; Myra who found schooling oppressive and left school at an early age, drawing instead on social networks (especially neighbors who migrated) to find an alternative recourse that eventually led to success; Maribel (self-proclaimed "wild girl") who left secondary school due to boredom, moved to a neighboring town, and learned to survive based on her social networks rather than on formal schooling, eventually marrying an American and living in the US where she wants her own children to be educated; and Nicole, a former classmate of Meyers at Seattle University who today is a successful attorney in the US and who credits all her successes to her family in Villachuato, not to her formal education despite her parents' own formal illiteracy. In sum, all six case studies of these women found that it was "interpersonal relationships that played an important part in their resistance, as exposure to other people's experiences or direct assistance from friends and family—increasingly expressed through domestic and international migration—became the means through which these women resisted oppressive forces in their lives and, in some cases, found alternative means to literacy" (110).

In chapter five, "'So You Don't Get Tricked': Counternarratives of Literacy in a Mexican Town," Meyers travels to the larger city nearby, Puruándiro, to show how literacy in Villachuato is viewed always as something that comes from someplace else. Students and residents of Villachuato have an unfinished library so research materials are inaccessible without traveling by bus to neighboring Puruándiro. Even there, the library is poor. This "autonomous thing"—literacy, travels from elsewhere and is something they are not a part of—it might visit periodically (like this foreign researcher did) but it is Other in all senses of the word. This sense of literacy as autonomous and outside their reality enables the citizens of Villachuato to take what Meyers again calls a "rhetorical stance toward literacy: enacting those elements that serve them, and resisting the rest" (116). This resistance as a rhetorical practice is "contextual, positional, and strategic" (116).

And of course international migration is a larger-than-life reality and influence in this rural town. More importantly for this study, it interferes with the state and nationalist message of public education, which is that its value is in realizing a national consciousness. So this tiny village has its own literacy crisis—and one that is a microcosm of others throughout rural Mexico. What Meyers calls "un choque de ideas" unfolds as we see teachers who speak of their students in ways that show they do not really understand how the disconnect between the curriculum and the values it imparts do not address the communities' real needs. Nor are the home knowledges and funds of knowledge the students possess ever permitted space in classroom discussions. Indeed, the idea of literacy as self-defense, as resistance, is the real crisis, the true counternarrative at play here.

What is literacy? And why is it useful to the citizens of a rural, non wage-labor economy? One thing that is obvious is that while literacy does not improve one's economic mobility, it often does improve one's cultural capital. For one thing, there is still shame associated with illiteracy. For another, in a village dominated by migration, the remittances sent home by its citizens permit the people of Villachuato to participate and to resist education according to their own needs. They can become agents of their own lives.

In chapter six, "'Like Going from Black and White to Color': Mexican Students' Experiences in U.S. Schools", Meyers follows the migratory path to Marshalltown, Iowa, where the Swift factory (the third largest hog-processing plant in the U.S.) employs 500 workers from Villachuato (figures from 2002). Here we see how the stakes of the literacy contract are raised. The promises of school are higher for these children of the migrants, but the commitment they seek is also more demanding (you need to assimilate). Literacy here begins to function as assimilation because it promotes cultural values in openly ideological ways. Meyers does an expert job in delineating the differences between "education" and *educación*—the former is very much foundational to US education and concerns itself with school issues like academic mastery of content; the latter, *educación* means something different to Mexican families. It is about behavior—the family's responsibility. So this division between behavior and academic work is a "distinction that continues to exist" and that "does bar a full conversion to U.S. approaches to learning" on the part of these immigrant students (144).

Meyers is deft at showing how teachers in the US are positively supportive of these students but at the same time are blind to ways the parents of these migrants resist full conversion to the US paradigm of learning. Teachers talk about the students' academic progress and struggles while parents keep asking "but are they behaving well?"—continuing to insinuate their own agency into what matters to them about their children—*educación* not education. In the end, the experience of attending school in the US does cause many students to accidentally assimilate or to resist assimilation. But they are also "profoundly ambivalent about fulfilling school demands and the literacy contract itself" (150).

Finally, in the concluding chapter, Meyers examines how literacy is changing in a transnational world. She notes that in Villachuato, formal education is not the "primary means to economic growth, rather education is the *result* of a family's financial success" (13). The skills taught in school, like the curriculum around it, are developed in urban centers far from the daily lives and needs of non wage-labor economies. They simply are not relevant to survival if you are a farmer or a migrant. At the same time, these migrants with all their remittances—financial and social—do represent new forms of social capital for a community like Villachuato, capital that can undo negative impacts of the lack of cultural capital.

In a compelling call to educators, Meyers ends by asking all of us to reconsider our notions about this literacy contract. No longer is it a "means to an end" especially for immigrants. The realization of this requires a shift away from the belief in the effects of the literacy contract. And this is profound, claims Meyers. It essentially asks us to open ourselves to a "new orientation," one that "negates the contract culture that has dominated our approach to education for decades" (158). Considering how literacy is structured by and for global economies, and how issues of transliteracy are emerging in this highly mobile global economy, it is time we take up Meyers' call to open ourselves to the multiple literacies of the world and to understand how migratory cultures affect us all. I heartily agree with Meyers that "transnational migration" is the "next horizon of literacy studies we need to consider" (36).

New Media Literacies and Participatory Popular Culture Across Borders
Bronwyn T. Williams and Amy A. Zenger, eds.
New York, NY: Routledge, 2012. 219 pp.

Reviewed by Jessica E. Slentz
Case Western Reserve University

When Gail Hawisher and Cynthia Selfe published their collection *Global Literacies and the World Wide Web* (2000), they set out to challenge a prevailing cultural narrative of the time—the "global-village narrative" (Hawisher and Selfe 1). This narrative naively saw the Internet as an equalizing force capable of "[transcending] current geopolitical borders" to create a "connected global community"(2). The essays of that collection focused on "local" and culturally specific literacy practices affected and necessitated by the worldwide web in different communities throughout the world. In doing so, they demonstrated the "*internationalness*" (3) of digital literacy practices, while at the same time showing that, rather than the Internet being a tool of global connectedness, it more often "ensures that differences based on socio-economic status, color, and power are maintained, exacerbated, and reproduced, rather than eliminated" (13). As such, they demonstrated how the sites and contexts of online literacy practices are "sites of social struggle and change" (13).

More than a decade later, Bronwyn T. Williams' and Amy Zenger's edited collection *New Media Literacies and Participatory Popular Culture Across Borders* (2012) offers a return to international sites of web-based literacy practices, this time examining how, in spaces of participatory reading and writing online, popular culture—most specifically western/American popular culture—"provides an obvious opportunity for far ranging and more democratic contact across cultures" (Williams 25). While the significance of this "contact across cultures" is the motivating force behind this collection, it does not denote a turn towards a sort of "global-village narrative." Instead, by using popular culture as the focus of inquiry, *New Media Literacies* investigates the myriad ways in which digital technologies, multimodal literacy practices, and popular culture together affect how people read, write, construct identity, negotiate power, and create meaning through texts, both within and across specific cultural contexts and sites of social change.

New Media Literacies and Participatory Popular Culture Across Borders is Bronwyn Williams' third volume on digital literacy practices, and the second that he and Amy Zenger have edited together (their first being *Popular Culture and Representations of Literacy* in 2007). *New Media Literacies* expands on current scholarship in the disciplines of New Media and New Literacy Studies to examine what exactly is happening when popular culture is not only read and internalized, but also when it is experienced and appropriated globally. Williams and Zenger, joining conversations on digital literacy set forth by Colin Lankshear and Michelle Knobel, hold that the "autonomous" model of literacy as a collection of skills that must be acquired for one to read and write is inadequate as it does not take into account the social processes, power structures and performances of identity that the practices of reading and writing are connected to. Organized into two parts, *New Media Literacies* first explores how popular culture texts are read, watched, listened to, rewritten, remixed, and appropriated by young people transnationally, and then examines the ways in which the appropriation of popular culture affects how identity is constructed and performed in online spaces.

In part one of *New Media Literacies*, "New Media Literacies Across Cultures," the authors address the importance of online literacy practices in the lives and educations of young people, often focusing on educational environments. In his chapter, "The World on Your Screen: New Media, Remix, and the Politics of Cross-Cultural Contact," Williams highlights the prevalence of media convergence in the development of adolescents' literacy practices. Williams cautions against a naïve idealization of the participatory practices—that is of re-mixing and textual poaching on the one hand and the unrealistic vilification of them on the other. New literacy practices, he argues, should be approached critically since "the connections between literacy and participatory popular culture has important implications for how literacy scholars think about language, literacy, rhetoric, identity, and pedagogy in an increasingly mobile and cross-cultural world" (19). Jessica Schreyer, in "Adolescent Literacy Practices in Online Social Spaces," narrows Williams' study by looking at these new literacy practices specifically in "virtual, transnational youth communities" (61), adding "gaming" and "social networking" to the list of new literacy practices enacted by youth online. In "Digital Worlds and Shifting Borders: Popular Culture, Perception, and Pedagogy," Sandra Abrams, Hannah R. Gerber, and Melissa L. Burgess also examine gaming in online spaces, this time investigating the applications that digital games might have in the classroom and in developing academic literacy.

Part two of *New Media Literacies*, "Constructing Identity in an Online, Cross-Cultural World," focuses on the identity of the reader and negotiated agency in online spaces. In this section, the authors examine ways in which some participatory literacy practices afforded by Web 2.0 problematize traditional notions of the public/private and local/national. Mohanalakshmi Rajakumar's "Faceless Facebook: Female Qatari Users Choosing Wisely" demonstrates how the public/private arena of the Internet, which is both open and public as well as private and "inside the home," complicates the ways that Qatari women construct identity and negotiate agency through their Facebook profiles. Many Qatari women, Rajakumar argues, use social networking as a way to express themselves in ways they would otherwise be unable to at work or at home, at the same time making careful decisions about the types of photos and language they use so as to remain within social conventions of their more local, physical communities. Rajakumar sees these conscious negotiations between the public and private and the construction and performance of identity not as markers of social pressure as some in the west might view them (133), but as a complex set of literacy practices that highlight the ways in which adolescents across the globe approach the creation of identity online.

This drawing of parallels between local literacy practices and global communities continues throughout the second part of *New Media Literacies*. It becomes clear that the "borders" of the book's title do not only refer to language barriers, or to physical and geographic spaces (Carpenter), but also to the societal "borders" of gender (Hellekson), sexual orientation (Vicars), and power hierarchies inherent in the creation of knowledge or of popular culture itself (Cubbison and Sharma et. al). What is argued throughout these chapters is that the literacy practices involved in these negotiations of identity and agency, while occurring in local communities, by their very nature transcend the local, making participatory literacy online a "transnational" practice.

An ambitious collection that sets out to explore the intersection of new literacy practices and popular culture on a global scale, *New Media Literacies and Participatory Popular Culture Across Borders* is a cohesive collection of work by scholars from around the world. Even considering the diverse backgrounds of its contributors, *New Media Literacies* does not have the sense of disjointedness that many edited collections often do. What *New Media Literacies* does, it does brilliantly. In addition to a comprehensive resource on adolescent literacy practices online, Williams and Zenger have put together a collection of work that highlights the exciting as well as challenging and "disruptive" (1) ways in which the conversation about participatory and convergence cultures has changed in a very short period of time. When Henry Jenkins wrote *Convergence Culture* (2006) he was acutely aware not only of the "digital divide" but also of the fact that the consumer/producers of convergence culture were "disproportionately white, male, middle class and college educated" (Jenkins 23). *New Media Literacies and Participatory Popular Culture Across Borders* shows us that the literacy practices identified by New Media and New Literacy Studies are expanding to include a more diverse demographic, and that the younger generation of transnational "digital natives" is starting to have not only greater access to new literacy practices but also a greater influence on media convergence. While gestures towards the "global-village narrative" that Hawisher and Selfe cautioned against underlie some of the discussions surrounding popular culture, Williams et. al largely recognize that "globalism" itself is complicated, and self-consciously refrain from assuming fixed definitions of or binary attitudes toward the implications of technological change. There is a very conscious tension throughout the collection between how the literacy practices being analyzed simultaneously reify cultural borders and points of social access as well as serve to break them down. It is because of this tension that I would recommend this collection as a nuanced and fascinating look into literacy practices online as sites of social change.

Works Cited

Hawisher, Gail E. and Cynthia L. Selfe, Editors. *Global Literacies and the World Wide Web*. New York: Routledge, 2000. Print.

Jenkins, Henry. *Convergence Culture: Where Old and New Media Collide*. New York: New York UP, 2006. Print.

Williams, Bronwyn T. and Amy A. Zenger, Editors. *New Media Literacies and Participatory Popular Culture Across Borders*. New York: Routledge, 2012. Print.

Street Sex Workers' Discourse: Realizing Material Change through Agential Choice

Jill McCracken
New York: Routledge, 2013. 276 pp.

Review by Angela Clark-Oates
Arizona State University

In *Street Sex Workers' Discourse: Realizing Material Change Through Agential Choice*, Jill McCracken explores how material conditions encountered by sex workers—realities that "are created and *dis*rupted by discourse and rhetoric" (xxviii)—have the potential to both deny *and* construct agential choice. To do this, she used an ethnographic design to embed herself within a community of sex workers as a method for asking questions and spending time "with women who exchange sex for money or drugs and the myriad people who come in contact with them" (191). Consequently, as a researcher and a self-identified advocate for sex workers, McCracken argues for more complex interpretations of the stories, ones that can lead to robust solutions to the systemic and individual traumas experienced by them. Through critical discourse analysis,
she disrupts the historical and cultural interpretations of sex workers, showing how these constructed realities have led to ineffective or limited solutions because they have historically been hindered by an over-reliance on the archetypal binary of victim/survivor. This binary obscures not only the kaleidoscopic meaning of these workers' lives, but also limits opportunities for responsible rhetorical agency, or what McCracken calls agential choice.

During the "multi-sited ethnography," McCracken conducted fieldwork in the Nemez community (a city in the southwest US whose name was redacted) for thirty months. As a participant-observer, she was more than a neutral researcher. McCracken built credibility and trust in this community. She volunteered for a social services organization, and after two years, she became an employee of an agency that worked with those who were "chronically homeless" (192). In these positions, she learned the systems navigated by sex workers, she participated in outreach and education, and she developed relationships with the clients who were seeking services. Consequently, her identity as researcher was not static as she moved between her positions as volunteer, employee, and researcher, gathering her corpus of data across three sites in the community: articles from three primary newspapers, interviews with public figures, and interviews with street-based sex workers. As a participant-observer in this multi-sited ethnographic study, McCracken lived her research, engaged in the possibility of what Freire calls the "dynamic movement between researching and acting on the results of the research" (30). And this movement between her positions as researcher, volunteer, and employee allowed her to examine "the relationships between and among people and institutions that exist locally, globally, and internationally" (192).

McCracken organizes the book into six chapters, sandwiched by a preface and four appendices. The preface functions as an introduction to the research purpose, site, participants, and approach. She also introduces key concepts and terms that anchor her analysis in chapters two through five. In chapter one, she unpacks the theoretical framework, situating the reader in relation to the term *agential choice*, which is McCracken's foundational concept in the book. In chapter two and three, she examines the status of victimhood in relationships between the sex workers and the community. She goes on to identify various constructions of victimhood, to identify how these constructions get positioned as problems, and finally to explore how these constructions of victimhood and their corresponding positions limit proposed solutions. Chapter four explores the flaws of one particular solution: the individual responsibility and choice to change. Much like her critiques in chapter two and three of the problem/solution dichotomy, McCracken illustrates the failure and humiliation of a solution steeped in an ideology of individualism and self-reliance, which ignores the historical and cultural practices of traumatizing bodies marked as sex workers. In chapter five, she explores this systemic violence. McCracken writes, "...when systemic issues related to poverty and violence are at the root of many of the choices this individual has made, it is unfair to simply place the total responsibility on her shoulders and expect her to change" (125). In chapter six, she shares the implications of her research, focusing on systemic change, agential choice, and a re-imagining of individual change. In the appendices, McCracken provides access to the research artifacts: detailed descriptions of the participants, the research design and processes of analysis, data tables, and interview materials and protocols.

In chapter one, McCracken orients the reader to the theoretical tapestry that undergirds her study. She explains that meaning/truth (and thus material realities) are constructed at the intersection between the improvisation of experience and the fixed discursive representation of that experience. Relying on Judith Butler, McCracken argues *that* these patterns of meaning—difference through repetition—have the potential to shift based on the discourses and identities being used to construct them. She writes,

> I explore how the idea, term, identity, and material reality of 'the prostitute' is constituted in the discourse surrounding women who exchange sex for money or other gain, and then, as the places for disruption are revealed, explore how materialities can be made differently. (8)

And it is this theoretical point—the potentiality of discourses to shift fixed understandings of terms and experiences—that allows McCracken to explore the possibilities and constraints of *agential choice* for the street-based sex workers, but to do this, McCracken also relies heavily on Marilyn Cooper's theoretical notions of agency. And while I commend McCracken for attempting to use a framework that emerges from both Butler and Cooper's theoretical ideas of agency, she does not sustain this theoretical blending throughout the book. Instead, the scope of her research influences McCracken to rely much more on Cooper's notion of rhetorical agency, particularly Cooper's emphasis on "embodied individual agency" (qtd. in McCracken), a decision that proves useful in the last chapter of the book. But her brief exploration of the theoretical tension between Butler and Cooper opens up an important space that creates opportunities for further exploration by anyone interested in the rhetorical agent.

Although chapter one is theoretically dense, at the end, McCracken steps out of this theoretical space and writes directly to the readers, nudging them to be open-minded as they enter into this relationship with the text. McCracken encourages the readers to be responsible rhetorical agents who can shake their preconceived notions and stigmas and who can construct interpretive spaces that allow for agential choice. This subtle address of the reader is a meta-moment that hints at the vulnerabilities of being a researcher and a writer. And although this builds intimacy with the reader, McCracken uses this crafting technique very sparingly throughout the book. There are only two other places (in chapter two and chapter six) where she risks exposing these vulnerabilities, but in all three instances, McCracken builds ethos that ultimately persuades the reader to be the kind of listener, "who places trust in the individual, or other, believing she or he is doing her or his best" (12).

In chapter two, McCracken identifies two potential victims: the sex worker and the neighborhood where the sex workers reside. Through the analysis of newspaper articles and the interviews with public figures, she determines that the neighborhood, more than the sex workers, is constructed as being victimized by the drugs, violence, crime, and disease associated with street-based sex work. Inevitably, the construction of neighborhood as victim perpetuates the criminalization of the sex worker, an idea she explores more thoroughly in the third chapter. The logic of this solution is based on the premise that if the sex workers were removed from the neighborhood, the drugs, violence, crime, and disease would disappear. McCracken not only critiques this solution for its faulty logic, but also for its disproportional and detrimental impact on "people of color as well as transgender individuals" (24). She then explores the construction of sex worker as victim. And although McCracken's analysis across her corpus of data reveals the complex material conditions faced by the sex workers—poverty, abuse, trauma, neglect—the victim status is most often attributed to individual choice instead of these systemic conditions. In ignoring the systemic conditions, the newspapers, public figures, and even the sex workers themselves construct the sex worker as victimized by their own personal choice of substance abuse. She claims that in the corpus of newspaper articles that the cluster drugs/prostitution "occurs 157 times" (38). This evidence, triangulated with the interview data from the street-based sex workers and the public figures, reveals a strong correlation between drug use and prostitution, but McCracken interprets this finding through a critical lens, explaining how this cluster actual reveals the power of ideology and its embeddedness in our language: "Ideology is powerful, and an ideology of personal responsibility is emphasized in the language surrounding street-based sex work" (54). While McCracken's conclusion echoes the theoretical framework she constructs in chapter one and allows her to articulate this important finding, the readers would benefit from a more explicit connection as they navigate the ambiguous space between what the data reveals and what McCracken "sees" through the theoretical frame.

In chapters four and five, McCracken explores the limited opportunities of choice that sex workers are offered in relation to their marginalized position within the community. She critiques the hyper-individualism perpetuated in the victim/survivor dichotomy, illustrating how it perpetuates systemic violence. More importantly, McCracken thoroughly examines the relationship between language, power, and ideology, advocating for language that values instead of demeans the sex worker, that disrupts the status of victimhood instead of perpetuates it, and that acknowledges systemic issues related to sex work instead of obscuring them. In these chapters, McCracken shows her penchant for residing in the messy space between individual agency and systemic determinism, and in doing so, asks valuable questions about how policies and laws further stigmatize and criminalize vulnerable and marginalized populations, like sex workers, by dehumanizing their bodies and ignoring their voices.

Finally, in chapter six, McCracken crafts the dénouement. She argues for "developing an ideology and practice of power-with" in relation to sex workers, a practice that has the potential to create and respect *agential choice*. The term agential choice coined by McCracken is integral to the solutions she proposes to "begin modifying the discourse and ideologies surrounding the exchange for money and drugs" (161). At the end of this chapter, the author provides practical application for this theoretical concept. While I do find this new term useful is in thinking about how the reader, the police officer, the volunteer, or any other community service worker or community member can open more opportunities for sex workers to have agential choice, I am concerned by the limitation of discussing agency (particularly in relation to marginalized groups) as being dependent on the willingness of another to shift her actions, discourses, or ideologies through recognition of/by others. McCracken admits throughout the book that power influences who speaks, recognizes, and listens. The strength of her analysis, with its focus on language and ideologies, lies in her commitment to consistently acknowledge that power always, already exists between speaker and listener, and for her participants, there have been very few moments where they have been the speaker, positioned as a legitimate agent who can be trusted to make their own best choices (151). Yet, when McCracken discusses agential choice in the last chapter, she moves the focus from the sex workers to those community members with whom the sex worker is likely to interact. As a reader, I was surprised that she was unable to show how shifts in the sex workers' own discourses and ideologies might also contribute to more opportunities for agential choice. Instead, her practical applications are more of an outline for those who make policies and laws, work at rehabilitation and social service clinics, enforce the criminalization of this trade, and stigmatize the women, all of whom reside on the periphery of the lives of street-based sex workers. Although it is evident that this was an intentional decision that emerged from "what was contained and revealed in the interviews and corresponding analysis of specific material conditions" (166), I think McCracken's choices in this chapter imply an important question for other researchers interested in the rhetorical agent: How do researchers explore studies about ideologies, power, agency, and identities of stigmatized groups and provide practical implications for communities without privileging those who are already empowered by normative, cultural practices? This is not a flaw in McCracken's work. Instead, it is an acknowledgement of the vulnerabilities of being a researcher and writer who is concerned with understanding how individuals can change within systemic (almost obscure) constraints, an acknowledgement that McCracken does not shy away from in other chapters in the book. McCracken's research transcends the field of rhetoric, providing insight for sociologist, anthropologists, social workers, and criminologists. Moreover, by outlining agential ways of knowing and interacting with street-based sex workers, McCracken has ensured that her research has important theoretical and practical implications for community literacy studies. Like all relevant research, McCracken has opened up a space for further inquiry.

Works Cited

Freire, Paulo. "Creating Alternative Research Methods: Learning to Do It by Doing It." *Creating Knowledge: A Monopoly? Participatory Research in Development.* Eds. Budd L. Hall, Arthur Gillette, and Rajesh Tandon. New Delhi: Society for Participatory Research in Asia, 1982. Print.

PARLOR PRESS
EQUIPMENT FOR LIVING

Congratulations to These Award Winners & WPA Scholars!

The WPA Outcomes Statement—A Decade Later
Edited by Nicholas N. Behm, Gregory R. Glau, Deborah H. Holdstein, Duane Roen, and Edward M. White
Winner of the Best Book Award, Council of Writing Program Adminstrators (July, 2015)

GenAdmin: Theorizing WPA Identities in the Twenty-First Century
Colin Charlton, Jonikka Charlton, Tarez Samra Graban, Kathleen J. Ryan, & Amy Ferdinandt Stolley
Winner of the Best Book Award, Council of Writing Program Adminstrators (July, 2014)

Mics, Cameras, Symbolic Action: Audio-Visual Rhetoric for Writing Teachers
Bump Halbritter
Winner of the Distinguished Book Award from *Computers and Composition* (May, 2014)

New Releases

First-Year Composition: From Theory to Practice
Edited by Deborah Coxwell-Teague & Ronald F. Lunsford. 420 pages.

Twelve of the leading theorists in composition studies answer, in their own voices, the key question about what they hope to accomplish in a first-year composition course. Each chapter includes sample syllabi.

A Rhetoric for Writing Program Administrators
Edited by Rita Malenczyk. 471 pages.

Thirty-two contributors delineate the major issues and questions in the field of writing program administration and provide readers new to the field with theoretical lenses through which to view major issues and questions.

www.parlorpress.com

www.ingramcontent.com/pod-product-compliance
Lightning Source LLC
Chambersburg PA
CBHW031403160426
43196CB00007B/872